Praise for *Theological Reflection across Religious Traditions*

"The combination of practical wisdom, theological creativity, and theoretical sophistication that Foley brings to bear on the increasingly important issue of how one conducts theological reflection in an interfaith context is as singular as it is remarkable." —**Scott C. Alexander**, Catholic Theological Union

"Internationally recognized practical theologian and liturgist Edward Foley provides an invaluable resource for learning the practice of reflective believing—a crucial capacity for those who seek to lead and live alongside neighbors of diverse religious traditions. This is an excellent resource for ministers and people who are grappling with how to live authentically within their traditions and remain open and hospitable to those in theistic and non-theistic traditions. Foley transforms the well-known method of theological reflection and moves us beyond interfaith dialogue and interfaith theological reflection to a new practice: reflective believing." —**Kathleen A. Cahalan**, Saint John's University School of Theology and Seminary

"Foley has written a 'savory stew' full of imaginative metaphors and multiple methods of faith sharing and collaborative conversation that support a more inclusive way of theological reflection he calls 'reflective believing.' Foley invites us to 'watch our language in the presence of the other' to ensure that all views are heard and welcomed with appreciative respect and 'holy envy.' The book itself is a 'hospitable portal' through which readers with varying beliefs may enter confident that their spiritual and religious particularities will be respected." —**Herbert Anderson**, professor emeritus of pastoral theology, Catholic Theological Union

Theological Reflection across Religious Traditions

The Turn to Reflective Believing

EDWARD FOLEY

ROWMAN & LITTLEFIELD
Lanham • Boulder • New York • London

Published by Rowman & Littlefield
A wholly owned subsidiary of The Rowman & Littlefield Publishing Group, Inc.
4501 Forbes Boulevard, Suite 200, Lanham, Maryland 20706
www.rowman.com

Unit A, Whitacre Mews, 26-34 Stannary Street, London SE11 4AB

British Library Cataloguing in Publication Information Available

Library of Congress Cataloging-in-Publication Data
Foley, Edward.
  Theological reflection across religious traditions : the turn to reflective believing /
Edward Foley.
     pages cm
  Includes bibliographical references and index.
  ISBN 978-1-4422-4718-5 (cloth : alk. paper) — ISBN 978-1-4422-4719-2 (pbk.
) — ISBN 978-1-4422-4720-8 (electronic) 1. Religion. 2. Theology. I. Title.
  BL48.F56 2015
  202—dc23   2014043554

Printed in the United States of America

To James and Evelyn Whitehead,
generous mentors,
thoughtful colleagues,
enduring friends

Contents

Acknowledgments

There have been so many individuals, groups, and institutions that have contributed to the development of this project that writing these acknowledgments feels a bit daunting. The drafting of this work was a sabbatical project, and over the fifteen months that I was away from teaching and committee work, I had the privilege of speaking with literally hundreds of colleagues and consultants who shaped my thinking in ways that I yet do not fully comprehend. Catholic Theological Union granted the sabbatical for the 2012–2013 academic year, which was funded by a generous sabbatical fellowship from the Lilly Endowment and the continuing support of my religious community, the Capuchin Province of St. Joseph. For those gifts I am very grateful.

James and Evelyn Whitehead have been steady dialogue partners and friends who prodded and supported this reimagining project that had deep roots in their own groundbreaking work. Multiple colleagues at Catholic Theological Union read drafts of the book and offered useful input. I am particularly grateful to Professors Scott Alexander, Dianne Bergant, Stephen Bevans, Richard Fragomeni, and John Pawlikowski. Professor Tom Beaudoin of Fordham University has been a consistent support and source of valuable advice on the project. Through the kindness of Joshua Stanton and Honna Eichler from the State of Formation project, I received rich feedback from new colleagues, particularly Lucinda Mosher of Hartford Seminary, who in turn introduced me to generous voices such as Andree Grafstein from the Spiritual Life Center in West Hartford, Connecticut.

Professor David Hogue arranged a smart consultation with D.Min. students at Garrett-Evangelical Seminary, while Rabbis Larry Hoffman and Kim Geringer invited me to share a very fruitful retreat with the Tisch Rabbinical Fellows of Hebrew Union College and the alums of that program. Dr. Emily Click orchestrated a stimulating two-day consultation at Harvard Divinity School that included students, faculty, administrators, field supervisors, and leaders of their "meaning making" seminars. Colleague and writing partner Professor Herbert Anderson convened the practical theology group at the Graduate Theological Union in Berkeley for a very helpful conversation as the book was being drafted. In a more sustained way, the Collegeville Seminar on Integration coordinated by Professor Kathleen Cahalan of St. John's University has become a community of new learning and enduring friendships on this journey. Professors Rebecca Slough of the Anabaptist Mennonite Biblical Seminary and David Jenkins of Emory University were particularly engaged.

While teaching and lecturing in the Philippines during early 2013, several former students designed opportunities for eye-opening conversations and input. I am especially grateful to Sr. Dr. Tammy Prado, OSB, then president of St. Scholastica College in Manila; Dr. Lilith Usog, chair of the women's studies program at St. Scholastica; and Rev. Dr. Reu Galoy, OFM, academic dean of the Inter Congregational Theological Center in Manila, for their many kindnesses. Particularly rich was the dialogue they arranged with members of the Ecumenical Association of Third World Theologians. More recently, Mr. Brendan Dowd invited me to share my work with his colleagues at the Niagara Foundation in Chicago, who have become great interlocutors.

These many gatherings were punctuated by face-to-face, Skype, and e-mail conversations with other key voices in the development of this project. They include Cassie Meyer and Dr. Eboo Patel of the Interfaith Youth Core; Chris Stedman, the assistant humanist chaplain at Harvard University; Dr. Patricia O'Connell Killen, academic vice president at Gonzaga University; Professor Thomas Groome of Boston College; and Professor Cynthia Lindner from the Divinity School at the University of Chicago.

To the many collaborators who have given so generously—especially students past and present at Catholic Theological Union—I am most grateful. This has been an often exciting, sometimes daunting new path for me to travel, but one that care and friendship from so many has richly nourished and sustained.

Introduction

Shaping Leadership for Shifting Times

In all chaos there is a cosmos, in all disorder a secret order, in all caprice a fixed law, for everything that works is grounded in its opposite.

—*Carl Jung (1959, 32)*

In the coming pages I will make references to Olympic gold medalists and ancient Greek philosophers, celebrated comedic geniuses and former students, distinguished theologians and even some of my family members. From the beginning, I hope readers recognize that this work is not intended to be an exercise in esoteric religious theories or abstract intellectual pursuits. Rather, it has been conceived, designed, and written as a book for those interested in the practice of the reflective arts. In service of that purpose, I have been somewhat shameless in borrowing ideas and images from any and every source—no matter how apparently unconventional—to aid every reader, wherever you are on your own journey into the practice of what I have come to call and will eventually define for you as *reflective believing.*

Lee Hock (b. 1929) is one such unorthodox resource. His is not a name you might recognize, but, on the other hand, if you are familiar at all with the VISA logo, you already know some significant things about him. Hock is a financier, an organizational maverick, and one of the most successful CEOs in US history. In the late 1960s, he was a thirty-eight-year-old banker at an institution that was invested in the very first credit card—BankAmericard—then on the verge of collapse. Hock participated in a rethinking of that organization. That reimagining gave rise to a new corporation with Hock as its CEO: a company eventually renamed VISA International. As widely reported by people such as M. Mitchell Waldrop (Waldrop 1996), since that rebirth in 1970, VISA International has grown by roughly 10,000 percent and consistently expanded at roughly 20 percent per year. Even with the collapse of global financial markets, in the new millennium it is still consistently showing double-digit growth. It now operates in over two hundred countries worldwide, serves over half a billion clients, with annual sales that frequently surpass one trillion dollars. Not only did Hock make a great deal of money for himself and many others in this process, but he also completely reconceived leadership: first for business, and then for nonprofits, the public interest sector and even volunteer organizations. Such reimagining is the stuff of legends, which is why Hock was inducted into the Business Hall of Fame as well as *Money* magazine's hall of fame. Maybe he has something to say to leaders in the reflective arts as well.

In his reliance on inspirational sources as diverse as Lao Tse and Jeffersonian democratic ideals, Hock has both empirically demonstrated and persuasively reasoned that the dominant forms of leadership operative in his world are not only problematic but also destructive. He summarizes that

> hierarchical command-and-control pyramids of power, whether political, social, educational, or commercial, were aberrations of the Industrial age, antithetical to the human spirit, destructive of the biosphere, and structurally contrary to the whole history and methods of physical and biological evolution. They were not only archaic and increasingly irrelevant, they were a public menace. (Hock 1995, 8)

Keenly aware of such command-and-control frameworks, Hock worked for organization after organization in over fifteen years of what he characterized as guerrilla warfare. He likened his work to that of a sheep committed to unorthodox innovation and the successes they brought in the face of companies lead by lions intent upon corralling the sheep. Each time he was corralled, even though he had grown the company financially, Hock ended up feeling like a "hunk of unemployed mutton" (Hock 1995, 6). To his amusement, each of those organizations has since ceased to exist. Through this warfare Hock honed his craft—both practices and theories—that gave rise to what he eventually dubbed "chaordic leadership." He developed this new model because he believed that, even though companies and industries had clearly grown over two hundred years, there has been virtually no new or imaginative reconceptions of business (or other) organizations since the concepts of corporations emerged centuries ago. Given the revolution that was taking place in global markets and multinational competition, Hock fiercely believed that it was time for the eighteenth-century Enlightenment models to give way to something more edgy and contemporary.

Chaordic is a term that Hock used publicly for the first time in 1993: a newly minted modifier, forged from the words "chaos" and "order." This was Hock's after-the-fact attempt to name an honest and self-effacing approach to leadership—tested over decades—that attempted to invite order in the midst of chaos without imposing, prescribing, or predicting what that order should look like. Chaos theory is familiar to anyone who has seen the science fiction classic *Jurassic Park*. One of the lead characters in that movie was a self-described "chaotician" by the name of Ian Malcolm who warned against the attempt to harness the genetic power that allowed for the scientists of Jurassic Park to clone dinosaurs. Malcolm predicted the unpredictable and suggested that the island was an accident waiting to happen. While he could not forecast how it would happen, Malcolm was right, and the movie ends with the island in complete and utter chaos.

In a lighter vein, in chapter 5 we will consider the comedic genius of Robin Williams. The host of a popular television program once described interviewing Williams as something akin to confronting electricity with a butterfly net. Analogously, a chaordic form of leadership recognizes that it only has a butterfly net while it is attempting to at least lead, if not harness, the electric dynamic of any human community.

WHY REFLECTIVE BELIEVING?

Admittedly, the phrase "reflective believing" is nowhere as inventive as "chaordic." That should not be surprising, since I have never generated even a fraction of a fraction of a trillion dollars and am in no one's hall of fame. On the other hand, I find enormous resonance between Lee Hock's iconoclastic rethinking of business leadership and my admittedly "advanced beginner" attempt to rethink theological reflection in this twenty-first-century US context.

TEXTBOX I.1

A SAMPLE DEFINITION OF
THEOLOGICAL REFLECTION

"Theological reflection is a constructed, ordered, reflected en-
quiry into the interaction of one's self (person and role) and
one's context (God, the world and the neighbor) which produces
a conceptual framework which leads to action." (Carr 1997, 118)

My first experiences of what has traditionally—though inadequately—
been called theological reflection (or TR) were in the early 1970s. I was a
candidate for ordination in the Roman Catholic Church and was required to
do field placements as part of my ministry training. My first task was to visit
local grocery stores in Milwaukee and try to document whether the lettuce in
those stores was harvested by the United Farm Workers (UFW), an organization founded by civil rights activist Cesar Chavez (d. 1993). If it was not,
we tried to persuade the store owners or managers to take a stand for justice
and only sell lettuce harvested by the UFW. In doing so, we argued that they
would be supporting more humane conditions for the tens of thousands of
migrant farm workers then laboring in appalling conditions.

After these on-the-ground exercises, we gathered together as students and
mentors for "sharing" sessions in which we talked about our experiences and
what they meant to us, the UFW, and our theologies. We did not have a name
back then for the unsystematic processes we employed in our sharing; we just
did it. In the coming years it acquired a name among Christians, particularly
those engaged with training future ministers. It was called theological reflection, often shorthanded as TR. Appendix 1 of this book documents some of
that history, in the outlines of various "classic" forms of TR that developed in
the late twentieth century.

Somewhat akin to the chaotic changes in business and industry that took
place in the late twentieth century, theological education and the many ministries it was designed to serve have also undergone their own revolutions.
No longer the exclusive terrain of dominant culture males appointed to well-

established congregations, today's seminaries and divinity schools are admitting women in large numbers, some of whom represent growing populations of Jews, Muslims, Buddhists, and even secular humanists. Besides a marked diversity of ministerial students in gender and sexual orientation, ethnic background, and religious identity, the contexts in which such spiritual leaders and chaplains are exercising their service is enormously varied. Steeple churches and other traditional brick-and-mortar settings are giving way to ministries and services variously described as liquid, emergent, experimental, and avant-garde. It is clearly a chaordic age for ministers and chaplains of every stripe.

Not only does this new complexity and ordered chaos call for freshly imagined leadership, but it also challenges those of us in the formation of spiritual leaders, whatever its genre, to provide new frameworks for reflecting upon that leadership that are equally visionary and liquid. This work is my fledgling effort to respond to that challenge. As I will try to explain in the pages that follow, *reflective believing* is my attempt to provide effective, yet intentionally ambiguous, language for naming this evolving concept. The term is probably inadequate, but, as we will explore in chapter 2, all language is limited given the diversity of human experience and the quest of some to broach the transcendent. More than exploring the "language game" of reimagined theological reflection, however, this modest work also tries to map something of the current chaordic context, consider the many purposes for engaging in reflective believing, place reflective believing in dialogue with the wider issue of integration so central to theological education, and finally offer a framework for considering the various stages and tasks for becoming a competent, if not proficient, reflective believer.

WHERE TO BEGIN?

In my previous writings, I always presumed that the reader would begin with a book's introduction and then slowly work her way through each chapter in sequence until arriving—in desperation or delight—at the final chapter. That process might be one that you, as a reader, find useful. If so, just follow the numbered pages. On the other hand, there are other ways to exploit this resource that might be more chaordic and yet useful. If, for example, you as a reader have never studied any systematic form of theological reflection (see textbox 2.1), you might want to begin with appendix 1. There I have presented short synopses of four well-respected forms of TR, along with a fresh reimagining of TR by a respected former student and now colleague of mine. Reading all or some or one of those outlines might prompt you to put this book down and pursue one of those models first. If that is what you need, that is what you should do.

The first chapter is both a personal and a professional *apologia* that explains in more depth why and how this book developed. In the process, it also attempts to map more fully something of the chaordic context for ministry and spiritual leadership in the present age. If you have limited exposure to the breadth and diversity of ways of believing and leadership in those various paths, then chapter 1 might be a useful starting point. I have chosen to write this work in a strong first-person narrative and so freely recount experiences and encounters—effective as well as catastrophic—that have shaped me in this journey. If that piques your interest, then launch into chapter 1.

Chapter 2 is a consideration of the languages of reflective believing, broadly construed. This entails some consideration of the limits of our languages and the tolls they sometimes inadvertently extract from our dialogue partners. Employing the rich concept of "language games" from the philosopher Wittgenstein, I suggest that reflective believing is a distinctive language game with its own rules. I also try to look beyond the "words" and consider silence, body language, and ritualizing as powerful language components in this new game.

Others might be more interested in the various purposes and situations that reimagined theological reflection serves. Chapter 3 endeavors to illustrate some of that diversity, much of which was revealed to me in the many consultations with students and leaders in the reflective arts that shaped my writing over the past two years. If you have some experience in TR, you might want to begin with this chapter and place your own purposes and images of TR in dialogue with the thirty-five purposes and three brief case studies outlined there.

If you have some responsibility for leading theological reflection in a school of ministry or some variation on that theme, you could be more concerned about the relationship between reflective believing and the entirety of the seminary enterprise. Chapter 4 is my attempt to consider that larger picture. One of the topics that has both interested and puzzled me over the past few decades is the very nature of "integration." It is a goal that many of our formation programs hold as the ultimate purpose of such endeavors, but one not always well described or explained. My approach to the integrating process is admittedly more liquid that most. Hopefully, it makes sense in this more chaordic environment in which this reimagined form of theological reflection endures as a key component, and contributes to your own thinking on the topic.

The final chapter borrows the framework of the Dreyfus brothers, which they developed for charting the progress of a practitioner from novice to expert. I have tried to wed their insightful work with the more ambiguous task of nurturing people in the reflective arts. Producing an expert in this arena is akin to growing a saint. I am not sure if or how such is possible. At the same time, the Dreyfus brothers' template strikes me as quite helpful in leading a novice in the reflective arts toward increasing competency and surety in that practice.

While print on a page, I have imagined this emerging work as a series of hyperlinked ideas and insights, resources and metaphors. Just as there is no one way to engage in effective and ethical reflective believing, so there is probably no one way to exploit the content here presented to you. Similar to the way I think about preaching, my goal here is to provide a sufficient number of credible and evocative "dots" so that you can connect them in a way that is helpful to your journey and beneficial to the communities that you do or will serve. In chapter 1 we will consider a form of thinking and conversing that is less linear and systematic and more fluid and open, sometimes called *rhizomatic*. While there is a clear progression throughout this book that you can follow on a more linear path if you wish, I also want both to respect and model the "rhizomatic" ideal that appears so promising and necessary in this age of growing diversity. However you decide to make this trek through reflective believing, I am profoundly grateful for your willingness to cultivate the reflective arts in service to your local communities and the wider human family in ways that are even beyond my imagining.

1

Believing from the Outside-In

When you're traveling, ask the traveler for advice
not someone whose lameness keeps him in one place.

—*Rumi (2004, 193)*

This project has not come to the end that was originally envisioned. It could be a sign that through my engagement with this process over the years some conversion took place and that something or someone changed my mind about this evolving topic. On the other hand, it is also possible that the unexpected turns in these writings merely indicate that I lost my literary or spiritual compass and produced a meandering hybrid of a resource. Readers will have to decide for themselves which is true. My instinct is that the truth lies somewhere in the gray between those two polarities. This is certainly not an end point in my journey into the topic and practice, but a speakable point—unquestionably not the last word (even for me) but hopefully ideas sufficiently cooked that they render this a useful word.

What may be most true for me on this journey into reflective believing is that I often asked travelers for advice. The first of these to advise me along this path were James and Evelyn Whitehead. Their wisdom initially came to me through reading their groundbreaking book *Method in Ministry,* and later many times over they lavished their wise counsel through enriching personal encounters. These Roman Catholic lay theologians charted with clarity and concision a pathway for Christian ministers—both the novice and the veteran—for reflecting upon their service through the eyes of faith (see appendix 1D). For many years I taught their model and method to a broad range of seasoned Christian ministers: women and men who were South African Pentecostals and Sri Lankan Episcopal priests, Korean Presbyterian pastors and Jesuits from India, Polish nuns working in Taiwan, and Baptist preachers from Milwaukee. These co-learners were also a rich fount of wisdom, as each from their very particular contexts pushed the boundaries of what we were then calling theological reflection.

Then a funny thing happened on that winding path some call enlightenment. The Ecumenical Doctor of Ministry program, which was the setting for much of this journey, accepted its first Muslim woman into the program: others would follow. When I look back on that experience, it seems as though we were given a shot of adrenalin as I and my co-learners found ourselves racing down a track as exhilarating as it was unfamiliar. It is true that we had previously admitted Christian students with significant ministerial experience in Muslim contexts: most often missionaries to Africa. Many of these individuals might be considered religiously "bilingual," comfortable and sometimes even fluent in diverse faith traditions and religious contexts. While they spoke Christian theology or Christian ministry as a first language, they were often adept at translating it into Islamic thought or the local Muslim context. One such student interested in "spirituality" recognized that "spirituality" was not a common category in Islam, but through study and dialogue came to understand that both traditions could speak about "mysticism." This "Christians pondering Islam" framework contributed to my personal and professional agenda of critiquing and expanding methods for theological reflection so that they became increasingly inclusive.

While it took over a decade to understand—not that I understand fully now—I slowly realized that this well-intentioned approach could be considered a form of colonialism. I was employing an admittedly widely celebrated Christian and Western framework as the platform for enabling theological reflection across landscapes that were increasingly non-Western and non-Christian. My naïve image was that of a progressively flexible and expanding interreligious form of theological reflection, but one in which the Whiteheads' framework—and thus a Western Christian perspective—was at its core (see figure 1.1).

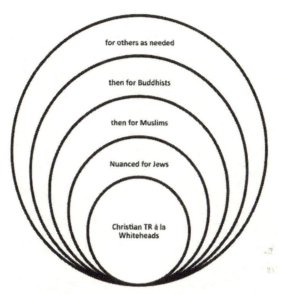

FIGURE 1.1.

In the language of Stephen Bevans, this could be considered a "translation" or "adaptation" model of contextual theology, in which the same seed is continuously replanted in different ground (2005, 37–53). While the fruit of this transplanting process may take on some of the tastes and ingredients of the local context, it is essentially unchanged by it. This "kernel and husk" tactic—one I unconsciously explored for many years—was limited by its many unspoken presuppositions. Primary among these was the assumption that some message, or in this case some process for theological reflection, was at its heart supracultural and supracontextual. Thus, one could suppose—mistakenly, of course—that this process could transcend the limits of any other belief system or worldview. It became increasingly clear, however, that somehow tweaking the Whiteheads' model and method would still not adequately respect the diverse spiritual, social, and cultural contexts of those many "others" who were interested in participating in the reflective arts. If there actually existed a path for spiritual dialogue that both supported and stimulated a mutually respectful conversation across the widely shifting contours of contemporary believing, then the metaphor of an "ever-widening circle" with a "Whiteheadian center" needed to be abandoned.

ENDLESS CIRCLES

A first instinct for correcting and replacing this "ever-widening circle" approach to TR was to add more circles. This decentralizing maneuver would, I thought, certainly unseat the privilege of any single perspective and move the conversation toward something more reciprocal. This is, for example, how I have previously understood and even experienced interfaith dialogue between the Abrahamic religions of Judaism, Christianity, and Islam. One of the presumptions of this approach is that there are some central beliefs or practices that are not only shared across these traditions but also central to them. A powerful example of this approach is the "Common Word" initiative between Muslims and Christians.

The spark for the "Common Word" initiative was a lecture delivered by Pope Benedict XVI at the University of Regensburg in 2006. In that lecture, the Roman Catholic leader included a denigrating remark about Islam and holy war from a fourteenth-century Byzantine emperor: "Show me just what Muhammad brought that was new, and there you will find things only evil and inhuman, such as his command to spread by the sword the faith he preached" (Benedict XVI 2006). A year later, 138 Muslim scholars and clerics responded with an open letter "to leaders of Christian churches everywhere" titled *A Common Word between Us and You.* In it they proposed that both Christianity and Islam share a central belief about loving God and loving one's neighbor. Many Christian church leaders and theologians spoke out in support of this statement, various conferences and workshops were convened, and multiple publications ensued.

The resulting dialogue between these two faith traditions—some of which could clearly be interpreted as forms of "interfaith theological reflection"—was rich and rewarding. It demonstrated in a remarkable way how common ground could be shared by two quite distinctive belief systems. No longer was this an attempt to fit one perspective inside another's circle. Rather, this was a complementary interchange of shared belief that was potentially enlightening for both parties. This form of respectful dialogue is precisely what the World Council of Churches embraces in its 1979 "Guidelines on Dialogue with People of Living Faiths and Ideologies."

While certainly an informed and respectful approach, this two-way exchange could also appear to be exclusionary. Even though Muslims and Christians together comprise almost half of the world's population, Jews could argue that it is their religious tradition that provides the foundational tenet of love of God (Book of Deuteronomy 6:5) and love of neighbor (Book of Leviticus 19:18), which serves as the meeting point for this "Common Word" dialogue. Both historically and theologically, therefore, one could contend that Judaism is a lynchpin for such a dialogue and cannot be excluded. The simple solution, of course, would be to add one more circle.

However, Buddhists could in turn argue that their religion is one of the most widespread in the world, twenty-five times more populous than Judaism. Care for one's neighbor, as expressed, for example, in the teaching "Whoever harms the harmless or oppresses the innocent and just is like a fool tossing dust into the wind—his wrongdoing will fly back in his face" (*Dhammapada* 1985, 67), is deeply reflective of a Buddhist ethic. This would suggest a fourth intersecting circle, except that it would have a more narrow common ground. Since Buddhism is not concerned with belief in a personal God, but is rather a spiritual path toward enlightenment, the common ground here would only be care for neighbor and not love of God.

The technique of simply adding more and more circles in an attempt to pinpoint some shared religious tenet or framework as the starting point for a reimagined form of what some have called "interfaith theological reflection" seems both inadequate and a strategic nightmare. How many interlocking circles would be necessary to hold in equal regard given the diversity of belief systems in the twenty-first-century United States: Ten? Twenty? Thirty? Forty?

A concrete example of this diversity is the intake form for Stanford University Hospital, which allows incoming patients to note their religious preferences (see textbox 1.1). The form lists forty religious options plus the possibility of selecting "Other religion," "No religious preference," "Patient declines to say," "Requests no chaplain visit," and "Unknown." This dizzying display of belief options suggests that no interlocking or overlapping framework intent on finding some universally agreed upon starting point for reimagined "interfaith theological reflection" can adequately address the religious polyphony that marks contemporary US society. One important variable here is not only the differing belief-frameworks but also the wildly different goals or reasons for which one engages in TR. This is a topic to which we will return in some depth in chapter 3.

It may surprise some to discover that besides people from "traditional religions," there are individuals who do not profess belief in any religion or

TEXTBOX 1.1

STANFORD UNIVERSITY HOSPITAL:
CATEGORIES OF "RELIGIOUS
PREFERENCES" FOR PATIENTS

1. Apostolic
2. Armenian
3. Assembly of God
4. Baha'i
5. Baptist
6. Bible Churches
7. Buddhist
8. Catholic
9. Christian
10. Christian Scientist
11. Church of Christ
12. Church of God
13. Church of Scientology
14. Episcopal
15. Greek Orthodox
16. Hindu
17. Jain
18. Jehovah's Witnesses
19. Jewish (Hebrew)
20. Latter-day Saints (Mormon)
21. Lutheran
22. Mennonite
23. Methodist
24. Metropolitan Community Church
25. Muslim
26. Native American
27. Nazarene
28. No Religious Preference
29. Other Religion
30. Patient declines to say
31. Pentecostal
32. Presbyterian
33. Protestant
34. Quaker
35. Religious Scientist
36. Requests no chaplain visit
37. Russian Orthodox
38. Seventh-day Adventist
39. Sikh
40. Stanford Memorial Church
41. Unitarian
42. United Church of Christ
43. Unity
44. Unknown
45. Wicca

do not hold for the existence of any god and yet who still want to engage in what they themselves sometimes call "interfaith dialogue." True, there are those participating in a *new atheist* movement who not only want nothing to do with religion but also are quite intent upon expending their considerable energies in trying to both debunk and destroy any and every religious system. The self described "anti-theist" Christopher Hitchens (d. 2011) has written a classic from this perspective. *God Is Not Great*, with its disturbing subtitle *How Religion Poisons Everything* (2007), is a powerful manifesto for some who want no dialogue with individuals or groups who invest in the religious or spiritual.

There are others, however, those who are not only interested in engaging in interfaith cooperation for the sake of advancing some common social program but also deeply concerned with sharing their personal stories and what could be construed as their own belief systems. Atheist and interfaith activist Chris Stedman exemplifies this approach in his memoir *Faitheist*. From his own experience and beliefs, Stedman is adamant in holding that "atheists and agnostics are more than just welcome in the interfaith movement: our role is important" (Stedman 2012, 131). How does one reimagine theological reflection so that it is hospitable to interlocutors like Chris Stedman, who are both interested in and committed to this engagement? Such a reimagining may be especially challenging to those of us from the Abrahamic religions who could too easily dismiss a dialogue of belief with humanists, agnostics, or even atheists as a fruitless endeavor.

One fundamental challenge in this exploration is grounded in the awareness that any framework for common discourse and every set of parameters for dialogue is also a form of gatekeeping: in order to walk metaphorically through this dialogic gate, one has to pay an admission price. In spiritual, religious, or belief-based communication, that price is often a willingness to engage in this interchange by employing some dominant form of discourse that, for many, is someone else's vernacular. Upon reflection, it seems that is precisely what I was doing in my halting attempts to invite Christians of many stripes as well as Muslims into the world of theological reflection as I understood it. The admission price into TR for our professional doctoral students was learning and employing the framework of the Whiteheads as a shared language. Slowly it dawned on me, however, that "speaking Whiteheads" was an inappropriate and probably unfair toll for the many who wished to engage in shared reflection about believing but for whom the Whiteheads' model was a challenging foreign language.

There will always be gatekeeping in every shared discourse. Maybe in any reimagined form of "interfaith theological reflection," however, those costs can be mitigated by the existence of not just one but many entry gates: each with a moderate toll. Instead of a single framework for such belief sharing like the Whiteheads, people interested in this endeavor may need to be increasingly flexible in recognizing the many possible avenues into this conversation. Creating more hospitable forms of TR will not result in conversational highways without cost or even sacrifice. A few years ago, in the midst of conversations with Jewish rabbinical and cantorial students about the potential demands of such discourse, one young woman brought the room to an unusual quiet when she suggested that in order for her to engage in such exchange, she may have to lay aside her belief that the Jews were God's only chosen people. There will be costs, tolls, and even sacrifices for any shared speaking in this mode. As we will consider toward the end of this book, there will also be necessary suffering. My instinct is that a conversation without such costs is probably a conversation not worth having. On the other hand, maybe the required tolls will be less about a vernacular of concepts or methods (e.g., the need for a contextual analysis of the situation in which the discourse is to take place, as Holland and Henriot stress [see appendix 1B]), and more about a vernacular of attitudes or values such as mutual respect or the willingness to honor our shared humanity. My own tradition made a dramatic embrace of such a vernacular when, in the *Pastoral Constitution on the Church in the Modern World* from the Second Vatican Council (*Vatican Council II* 1996), it stressed from the very beginning of that document that there is nothing truly human which does not affect and engage the disciples of Christ.

LIQUIDS, GINGER ROOT, AND THE INTERNET

Whether one considers the current age as postmodern, late modern, or employs some other label, we are certainly living in an era not only marked by a new diversity but also characterized by what might be considered hyperpluralism. Given this reality, we recognize the unlikelihood that any single framework or entry point can enable the sharing of belief across the diverse terrains that define twenty-first-century US society: the primary context for this writing. That does not mean, however, that the enterprise is doomed from the start. Nor does it suggest that each of us should simply remain in our own hermetically sealed religious silos where we can practice our distinctive forms of theological reflection for our own individual purposes without antagonizing or misinterpreting one another. Insights and practices of the current age across the spectrum of sciences, philosophy, and technologies suggest other ways.

In his millennial publication *Liquid Modernity*, for example, Polish sociologist Zygmunt Bauman characterized contemporary culture and society as *liquid* rather than *solid*. According to Bauman, solids have a tendency to hold their shapes, are resistant to change, and can be thought to hinder or even neutralize the impact of time. On the other hand, liquids that ooze, drip, and seep are not fixed in time and space and, like rivers and oceans, are in a constant state of flux (Bauman 2000, 2). Their trademark is their fluidity. Bauman employs this solid–liquid contrast to characterize what has been happening to contemporary society, suggesting that an earlier stage of modernity appeared more stable and was analogous to solids, while in late modernity the solids are melting and society is increasingly manifesting signs of liquidity. One striking example of such liquidity is the shifting perception of ethnicity and even race in this country. For example, Chicago has traditionally been a city of well-defined ethnic neighborhoods: Irish, Polish, Korean, African American, and so forth. According to the 2010 US census, however, the fastest growing self-identification in the United States is that of people who consider themselves mixed-race in any of its fifty-seven possible combinations.

British theologian Pete Ward has picked up this image in his thoughtful musings about a *liquid church*. Ward argues that "we need to shift from seeing church as a gathering of people meeting in one place at one time—that is, a congregation—to a notion of church as a series of relationships and communications" (Ward 2002, 2). Reimagining "interfaith theological reflection" as more liquid than solid, a series of relationships and communications rather than some closed process conducted within the confines of one's synagogue, church, or mosque, is a provocative and promising metaphor. Such liquidity seems necessary not only because of the widening range of individuals with their distinctive beliefs who want to engage in this process, but also because of the perceived problems with TR even within traditional Christian contexts. Many theological educators recognize the difficulties with and even resistance to the standard forms of theological reflection as they are taught in various ministry programs and seminaries throughout Western Christianity. The list of criticism and complaints about TR as compiled by British practical theologians Stephen Pattison, Judith Thompson, and John Green pointedly underscores such concerns (see textbox 1.2).

Pete Ward's image of a decentralized way of being church finds resonance with an image borrowed from the field of botany creatively employed by two late twentieth-century French philosophers. Gilles Deleuze and Félix Guattari utilized the category of plants known as "rhizomes" as a metaphor for thinking about contemporary culture and thought. A rhizome, such

CRITIQUES OF THEOLOGICAL REFLECTION

- TR is a technical term that is essentially mystifying, alienating and nonspecific.
- TR only has value as an academic concept.
- TR is not practical or useful in actually achieving anything in practice—it does not contribute tools or insights to ministerial work.
- It is removed from life and "academic" in the worst sense.
- TR produces a sense of anxiety and contempt because of its lack of specificity together with its being apparently very demanding.
- TR as taught does not draw on individuals' knowledge, strengths and ways of reflecting already—it is not student or person centered.
- TR methods are not flexible in trying to develop and validate different ways of reflecting what might reflect different characters, styles, and so forth.

Abridged from Pattison, Thompson, and Green 2003, 123.

as ginger root, is a type of root system that grows horizontally under the surface. Unlike trees, whose roots generally grow deeper into the earth while their branches ordinarily shoot upward toward the sky, rhizomes do not have a clear beginning and ending point like a top or a bottom. This suggests that they also do not have a necessary single starting point as does the mighty oak, whose taproot explodes downward from some seed. Nor do rhizomes have a final "goal" such as a culminating canopy or crown. Instead, rhizomes creep along under the surface erratically generating shoots above the ground and roots that dig down into the earth. Rather than having a single taproot developing from an originating seed that serves as the center of the plant, each chunk of a rhizome can potentially generate a completely new and independent root system.

From the viewpoint of philosophy, Deleuze and Guattari consider this "rhizomatic" approach as a fruitful way for pondering contemporary thought through a nonhierarchical framework that allows many avenues for entering and exiting a conversation. They reflect that "a rhizome has no beginning or end; it is always in the middle, between things, interbeing, intermezzo" (Deleuze and Guattari 1988, 23). They also characterize a rhizome as an "alliance"—but often an alliance of the unexpected. Borrowing a second image from nature—this time from biology rather than botany—they also ponder how very different species or organisms interact with each other to the mutual benefit of both. Their specific example of this unexpected mutuality is the wasp and the orchid. Scientists have observed that some forms of orchids can trick male wasps into pollinating them by "convincing" their buzzing friends that they are actually female wasps because of the shape of the inner flower and its ability to emit chemical odors similar to those of female wasps. Since the male wasp actually gets no benefit from this alliance, however, a better example of such mutualism might be the way certain plants provide food for chimpanzees, while chimpanzees in turn spread the seeds of the plants. If nature teaches us that there can be some level of mutuality between chimpanzees and berries, or the more poetic image of wasps and orchids, maybe shared reflections between humanists and Roman Catholics is not such a farfetched idea!

This rhizomatic turn to nature by Deleuze and Guattari has unusual resonance with Dee Hock's chaordic rethinking of leadership that we cited in our introduction. Nature itself, as exemplified in that ginger root, could be considered one continuous manifestation of the chaos and order that Hock perceived were part of the DNA of modern businesses and industries. While he did not appear to know about the work of Deleuze and Guattari, his image of chaordic leadership was an implicit rejection of what they might characterize as an arboreal approach to leadership with its top-down command and control biases. Rather, Hock's embrace of a style of leadership in the midst of the unpredictable and chaotic seems to underscore his rhizomatic instincts.

Resonant with mainstream strands of postcolonial theory (see textbox 1.3), this rhizomatic highway is not a binary: neither white nor black, yes or no, inside or outside. One advantage of the rhizomatic metaphor over postcolonial theory, however, is that postcolonial theory is ordinarily couched in a worldview that holds for groups of conquerors or colonizers as well as groups of colonized or the subjugated. Postcolonial theories in their varied forms have shattered any simplistic belief that knowledge or power only moves in one direction and the colonized or subaltern are without power or influence. At the same time, postcolonial analysis frequently has overtones of oppression, the misuse of power, and the marginalization of peoples. The rhizome as a botanical image does not seem to carry such baggage. As an organic image it can appear more neutral, devoid of many negative connotations, and seems poised to invite a more "appreciative" rather than contrarian stance.

Maybe an even more accessible image for nonhierarchical discourse in this digital age could be that of the Internet. Decentralized from its inception, the Internet is a network of networks that operates as the world's most expansive global communication system. Early in its development, the project was taken over by the US Department of Defense, which recognized that a decentralized design was essential in order to keep the system from shutting down in case of enemy attack. The diffuse nature of the Internet—an immeasurable array of hardware and software reaching to virtually every inhabited quarter of the globe—is continuously reaffirmed in the various struggles by governments and an array of national and international agencies to regulate this virtually nongovernable entity.

One advantage of the Internet metaphor over a rhizomatic one is the ability of each computer or "host" to choose how to access the Internet highway. There are innumerable online services as well as a wide range of commercial Internet service providers available throughout much of the free world. While each portal ordinarily has some cost or toll, the flexibility of portals and their ability to meet the varying needs of the host is a provocative model for reimagining theological reflection. A further advantage of this digital metaphor

TEXTBOX 1.3

"Postcolonial theory, often said to begin with the work of Edward W. Said, Gayatri Chakravorty Spivak, and Homi K. Bhabha, looks at literature and society from two broad angles: how the writer, artist, cultural worker, and his or her context reflects a colonial past, and how they survive and carve out a new way of creating and understanding the world." (Spivak 2005, 1859) is its ability to reflect how each individual host can select which sites to visit, which chat rooms to enter, and which messages to send. Ordinarily, these individual decisions do not necessarily have an impact on each other. Thus, I can message my musician friend about our favorite jazz recording while reading a subaltern blog about the newest development in postcolonial theory, which I know does not interest her. Engaging the other does not require that we all visit the same site, employ the same provider, or even know all of our dialogue partners.

Every metaphor, like every vernacular, has its downsides, and thinking about the Internet as a model for nonhierarchical discourse is not without its limitations. One common criticism of Internet users is that their surfing is very individualistic and self-serving. Furthermore, Internet communication can be a form of hiding or masking one's true identity, and the disconnected and decentralized nature of the Internet can prod its users into operating as disconnected, faceless "hosts." Such pitfalls have sometimes led to the denigration and even demonization of the Internet by some educators and religious leaders. There is widespread suspicion that the Internet cannot really be a source of connection or reflection, and maybe should be avoided—even as a metaphor for the inventive connectivity required for launching into what some call "interfaith theological reflection."

While there is undoubtedly some truth to the ways that the Internet can be misused, a more appreciative perspective is also possible. Tom Beaudoin's *Virtual Faith* was a prophetic work in this regard. In this pioneering exploration of the spiritual quest of Generation Xers, Beaudoin argued for how cyberspace could be a metaphor for the transcendent (1998, 87), as well as for how it had the potential to create "real" cybercommunities—even cybercommunities of faith (1998, 87–88). He cites examples of how the Internet can help organize relief for victims of natural disasters, or circulate protest petitions, or otherwise help move people's opinions and beliefs (Beaudoin 1998, 88). Consider, for example, the role of social media in fueling the many civil and human rights movements that marked the Arab Spring of 2011 or of responding to the devastating destruction in the Philippines in the aftermath of super typhoon Haiyan. Even though organization of the Internet is admittedly chaotic, unpredictable, and continuously in flux, it yet has the potential to contribute effectively to the common good and the up building of the human family.

On a more personal note, I recall my own participation in the wellness journeys of multiple friends by subscribing to their care pages on line. A particularly poignant memory recalls the journey of a young friend, Mikey, who was diagnosed with brain cancer at the age of ten. For five years a community of friends "gathered" on the Internet to offer support and prayers as he went through surgery and chemotherapy and experienced the joy of remission. We were also there when the cancer returned, all medical protocols failed, and the family held him close in hospice. Yes, many of us also saw Mikey face to face, touched him, ritualized with him, and kissed him good-bye. And when we did, we posted our experiences and stories so others could vicariously share in them. It was distressing for me that I could not attend his funeral and was out of the country for the final farewell offered by family and friends. The care page, with its tributes and touching remembrances, was an important link for me when I was thousands of miles away. Maybe the Internet is not only an effective metaphor for reimagining the chaordic nature of believing in a digital age but also a useful technology for the same.

THIS IS PERSONAL

There are many reasons why people reflect upon their beliefs, or engage in sharing the twists and turns of their journey into believing with others. In chapter 3 I will outline what I have learned from others about the many and varied goals for engaging in what traditionally has been called theological reflection. Before speaking about the goals and values of others, however, it seems necessary, and probably more honest, to set out some of the specific reasons why I think reimagining this process is important.

My reasons for undertaking this journey are not theoretical, but quite practical and deeply rooted in my own experiences. Those personal and professional experiences stretching over some decades both affirm the need for doing this kind of reflective work and underscore (for me) the problems with the traditional paths for such reflecting. While there are multiple reasons why I believe this reimagining is important, there are two that most immediately and persistently come to mind: my role as a theological educator and as a pastoral minister. While these will be treated here as distinctive reasons, they are neither separate nor unrelated to each other.

The first reason is directly related to my vocation as a theological educator. For over three decades I have had the privilege of teaching ministry skills in a graduate school of theology and ministry that has one of the most diverse student populations one could possibly imagine for such a school. It is a mix of women and men, some studying for ordained ministry in the Roman Catholic Church, while others prepare to work as lay ministers in church-related or not-for-profit positions. While there is no "average" year at Catholic Theological Union (CTU), during a recent school year we enrolled students from almost fifty countries: from Ireland to Iraq, from Chile to China. Sometimes identified as a "mission-sending school," our graduates currently serve in at least eighty countries around the world on every habitable continent. While we do have some Muslims and Christians of varying denominations enrolled at CTU, our population is overwhelmingly Roman Catholic. However, because of our cross-registration policy with ten other seminaries in Chicago (the Association of Chicago Theological Schools), and since we are located in the Hyde Park neighborhood with three of those schools and close to the divinity school of the University of Chicago, our classrooms are often more diverse than our school's own enrollees.

What spurs this inquiry for me as a theological educator is not only the richness of contexts and experiences that our students bring into our shared learning environment, but more so the growing diversity in faith expressions and belief systems that they will encounter in their future ministries, even if they stay within the United States. The inpatient checklist from Stanford University Hospital we referenced above is not some aberration, but an indicator of the new normal in the United States. That new normal is well exemplified in my own hometown, Chicago. In 1893, the first parliament of the world's religions assembled here, with representatives from every major and many smaller faith communities. When the hundredth anniversary of that gathering was held here in 1993, organizers noted that the world's religions were no longer coming *to* Chicago: they were already *in* Chicago, with sizeable communities of Hindus, Buddhists, Jains, Zoroastrians, Baha'is, and Muslims (Toolan 1993, 3). That diversity is only increasing. Recently the *Chicago Tribune* reported that there are over 176 religious traditions in Illinois, and Muslims are the third-largest group in the state (Brachear 2012).

Even this mapping of "religious" diversity does not provide a complete picture of the innumerable ways people in this country and my own city configure themselves around the issue of religion. While the number of self-professed atheists and agnostics in the United States remains small (about 6 percent), that number is growing. More dramatic are the number of "nones" or people, who when asked about religion, say they have "none." Their number now stands at about 14 percent of our total population, and a much larger percentage of those under thirty years of age in this country. Nones are not atheists: most of them report that they believe in God, and almost 20 percent of them say they pray every day (Pew Forum 2012, 9–10).

If about 20 percent of all adults in the United States are religiously "unaffiliated," with that percentage jumping to 32 percent of those who are under thirty years of age, how will future ministers "engage" with such an unavoidable number? While that might seem an odd question, the data demonstrates that most "unaffiliated" think that religious institutions help society especially by their work with the poor (Pew Forum 2012, 10). If Catholic priests and Christian ministers are going to engage seriously in building a just, tolerant, and peaceful society, we are necessarily going to have to collaborate with believers, the unaffiliated, and nonbelievers as well. Yet, since Roman Catholic ministers (both lay and ordained), like ministers from other traditions, are not simply social workers but are expected to be steeped in our religious heritage and committed practitioners of our inherited spiritualities, we also need to consider how we can bring our religious traditions to bear in this new world of collaboration and division. This has been a central concern for TR since its inception. What frameworks will we employ to seek common ground in values or spiritual insights without proselytizing or repelling those who do not share our belief frameworks? Beyond engaging in interbelief collaboration when lobbying for gun control or addressing the needs of the homeless, can we also engage in some reimagined form of theological reflection on these common ground ventures? Maybe more challenging, do we turn to the reflective arts only when we are back in our own spiritual silos, or are we capable of journeying into the mystery of reflective believing with the religiously defined other?

While my primary responsibility is as a theological educator, I am also a pastoral minister. Thus, my concerns about what my students will face in their ministry are deeply resonant with the challenges that I confront in trying to negotiate this shifting landscape of believing and nonbelieving. The most common way I exercise my ministry outside of teaching is preaching and leading public worship. I have the privilege of doing so at a large, bustling parish near the heart of Chicago. It is a place that welcomes longtime parishioners and visitors from the local hotels, the political elite, and the politically attuned, as well as young families and single young adults often drawn to the many social and social service events, including what is billed each summer as "the world's largest block party." It is estimated that on an average Sunday this parish welcomes visitors from approximately two hundred ZIP codes.

While I have no extensive empirical evidence to support it, I yet intuit that a significant minority of people who flock to worship at Old St. Pat's on a Sunday morning at least lean toward the "religiously unaffiliated" pole and would consider themselves "spiritual but not religious." Anecdotally, I know that they come for a variety of reasons. Sometimes they are home from college or a distant job placement and decide to accompany parents who are more regular church goers, or they tag along with friends who want to go to Old St. Pat's on St. Patrick's Day! Other times they come because of the high quality music and great hospitality extended through the ritual. And then there are those times, such as Christmas or Easter, when going to church just feels like the appropriate thing to do.

How do I preach in such an environment so that I do not further alienate this religiously marginalized minority? Data demonstrates that approximately one out of ten adults in the United States is a former Roman Catholic. I know that some of them do come to church, especially on the big feasts. If many, especially young adults, are exiting my church in growing numbers, how do I honor their presence and that of their unaffiliated friends when they do come to church for whatever reason? I consider preaching a public form of theological reflection: an attempt to make sense of life and world events in view of my own religious heritage, in the context of a sacred setting, punctuated by powerful music, rich ritual, and honored texts. Without pandering, I believe it is my responsibility to offer an interpretation of life that not only is richly meaningful for staunch Roman Catholic believers but also engaging for those who do not share my belief system. An ancient maxim in my tradition declares that "grace builds on nature." Without being a humanist, it makes sense for me to exercise the form of theological reflection known as preaching in such a way that—as previously suggested—it has a sufficient number of entry points or portals without outlandish tolls so that there is potential for the unaffiliated actually to have some connection with the preaching event.

In his eye-opening book, *Religion for Atheists*, Alain de Botton suggests that religion is designed to help people to live together in peace, and to cope with loss and death (see textbox 1.4). Whether one agrees with his assessment

"We invented religions to serve two central needs which continue to this day and which secular society has not been able to
solve with any particular skill: first, the need to live together in
communities in harmony, despite our deeply rooted selfish and
violent impulses. And second the need to cope with terrifying
degrees of pain which arise from our vulnerability to professional
failure, to troubled relationships, to the death of loved ones and
to our decay and demise." (de Botton 2012, 12)

or not, it is my experience that the two Roman Catholic rituals more than any others that draw people from across the belief spectrum into our churches are weddings and funerals. Both could be understood to address issues of harmony and loss. Weddings are not just about the couple but also about the multiple families that a married couple represents. Families marry families, and often that can be a source of conflict, especially when those families are marked by internal conflicts or divorce, or come from different ethnic, social, or religious contexts. Weddings are also about loss, whether experienced as daddy's little girl who has another man in her life or as the only son who now has to share his father with a new stepmother. How do I help interpret these experiences of harmony and loss for family and friends who increasingly do not share the same belief, much less any traditional belief system? This challenge is only magnified as more and more Roman Catholics marry people of other faiths and the unaffiliated.

More than weddings, the challenge of offering a credible interpretation of harmony and loss across the belief terrain is especially heightened at funerals. Recently, I presided at the funeral of a beloved nephew who was killed in a car crash at the age of thirty-three. Like many of his cousins and the friends who flocked to his funeral, he believed in Tolkien more than the gospels, and honored Gandalf more than Jesus. While Tolkien admitted that *The Lord of the Rings* was a deeply religious, even "Catholic," work, that is not always how it is read or experienced (e.g., through Peter Jackson's cinematic portrayals of the trilogy instead of through reading of the book). There are, however, deeply human themes in Tolkien's work that in their own rhizomatic way connect with a wide array of beliefs. It is a story about harmony and loss, about fellowship and death, about a vast array of creatures with particular forms of faith who join together on a common quest. While I could have offered a distinctly Roman Catholic interpretation of Michael's death through Tolkien, it did not seem to be what was needed in the moment or would have been well received. Thus, I was stretched to preach and preside in a different modality, hoping that there were enough hospitable portals in my thoughts and in my words so that brokenhearted family and friends in that room—representing a wide spectrum of faith perspectives—could experience some peace and consolation in their loss. At the suggestion of colleagues, I have included that "sermon" at the end of this book (appendix 2).

BELIEVING FROM THE OUTSIDE-IN

Early in this new millennium a group of activists established the "network of spiritual progressives." Their definition of being spiritually progressive does not presume that you believe in God or are part of some organized religion. Rather, it means a willingness to reject the "old bottom line," whose standards they believe were the maximization of money, power, and fame. Instead, spiritual progressives embrace a "new bottom line," whose standards are the ability to be loving, generous, and caring (The Network of Spiritual Progressives). One of the founders of that movement, Rabbi Michael Lerner, later wrote that in the current religious diversity, part of the new bottom line is the willingness to escape "the narrowness imposed by the demands of loyalty to our own religious or denominational institutions without breaking those ties completely" (Lerner 2009, 110). He goes on to note the value of affirming the particularities of each religious and spiritual tradition—without homogenizing them—in a way that allows for shared work toward a common good.

Lerner's vision has resonance with this exercise in rethinking theological reflection. As noted at the outset of this chapter, my previous bottom line for engaging in TR was employing a decidedly Christian and Western framework that I attempted to render more inclusive. It was a model of reflection that began on the inside of my context and faith and moved outward. Increasingly, however, I am convinced that the new bottom line for any reimagined theological reflection begins with respecting and honoring the other. This "outside-in" approach to reflective believing could also be a provocative frame for pondering the nature of mission for our communities of faith as we reimagine how to coexist and flourish in this increasingly diverse world.

Religious traditions such as my own do not always give the impression that they have anything to learn from other religions, particularly from humanists, agnostics, or atheists. We often operate as though we are the only light in the darkness and the only consolation amid the turmoil and suffering that daily surrounds us. Ironically, core teachings from my own tradition challenge such myopia. The great reforming Second Vatican Council (1962–1965), in no. 40 of its *Pastoral Constitution on the Church in the Modern World*, not only speaks about the Roman Catholic Church's need to contribute to human kind (*Vatican Council II* 1996, 207) but also admits that it has been helped by people of all classes and conditions. Its surprising teaching in no. 44 is that "whoever contributes to the development of the human community . . . is also contributing in no small way to the community of the church" (*Vatican Council II* 1996, 215).

Maybe more compelling and of infinitely wider appeal than a dogmatic statement from my church are the narratives of Jesus who continuously moved outside the circle of the religiously approved and socially acceptable in his forging a more inclusive image of the one he called God. What is especially startling in his ministry, as I read it, is that his outreach was not always and everywhere executed as a strategy of evangelization, and the litmus tests of its validity was not simply the drafting of new disciples. There is as much evidence in the New Testament that Jesus invited others to live in peace and charity with each other as there is that he specifically invited them to follow him. In Luke 17, he heals ten lepers but does not turn them into novices in his new band; instead, he sends them to be purified so that they could be incorporated back into Jewish society. In Mark 5, Jesus unknowing heals the woman with a blood flow, but rather than enlisting her as part of a new sisterhood, he sends her home in peace. In Mark 7, he raises to life the only son of the widow of Nain, but the gospels never indicate that mother or son ever became disciples. Instead, the text specifically notes that Jesus gave the son *back* to the mother rather than claiming him for his own.

My favorite Jesus narrative in this regard is about his encounter with the Syrophoenician woman in Mark 7 (see textbox 1.5). There is a parallel telling in Matthew, but Mark's version is not only earlier but also more unsettling. In this brief passage, Jesus appears to be off on his own, away from the disciples,

"From there he set out and went away to the region of Tyre. He entered a house and did not want anyone to know he was there. Yet he could not escape notice, but a woman whose little daughter had an unclean spirit immediately heard about him, and she came and bowed down at his feet. Now the woman was a Gentile, of Syrophoenician origin. She begged him to cast the demon out of her daughter. He said to her, 'Let the children be fed first, for it is not fair to take the children's food and throw it to the dogs.' But she answered him, 'Sir, even the dogs under the table eat the children's crumbs.' Then he said to her, 'For saying that, you may go—the demon has left your daughter.' So she went home, found the child lying on the bed, and the demon gone." (Mark 7:24–30, *New Revised Standard Version of the Bible*)

taking a break from the crowds and hiding out in the home of an unnamed ally when a stranger interrupts his retreat and begs him to heal her daughter. While many commentators have tried to clean up this story in which Jesus speaks quite harshly, Mark does not. He dares to depict a very human Jesus and paints a stark picture of this woman. She is a Greek, Syrophoenician by birth. She is not one of Jesus' people, but that should not surprise us, as Jesus has left the region of his birth and wandered into Sidon. This is her home, not his, and maybe he is a bit out of his depth and off his game. Yet she seems to know who Jesus is and begs him to heal her daughter. She is desperate and comes on strong. Some scholars claim that the only women who spoke to male strangers outside of their own homes were prostitutes: an interesting ploy, to treat people who are different from us as morally suspect. While Jesus does not treat her as morally suspect, he does seem to treat her as unworthy of his attention, his teaching, and his healing gift. So a resolute or maybe even stubborn Jesus meets an equally resolute and stubborn mother.

Jesus dismisses her initial request and seems to exclude her from the circle of God's children while chiding her for wanting to eat gifts destined for the chosen people. She is not fit to eat the food of these holy children, for she is no more than an animal. But this Syrophoenician woman is tough: the life of her daughter is at stake. So she picks up Jesus' words and hurls them back in his face, countering that even the dogs under the table can, do, and should eat the children's crumbs. So Jesus relents, but not because she made some great profession of faith or because of some sophisticated rhetorical argument or because of some appeal to Jewish law. Jesus seems to relent because she stands up to him and speaks the unvarnished truth as she sees it: there are crumbs aplenty, and surely enough left over from all the miraculous feeding Jesus had been doing to spare some for her and her daughter.

This hard-hitting and unusual gospel exchange seems to present Jesus as learning something new and doing an about-face. As recorded both by Mark and Matthew, Jesus is brought up short by an unexpected truth. Not only does he change his mind, but he does so in a breathtaking 180-degree turn. Most astonishing of all, it is a so-called pagan woman who is the catalyst for this change.

If Jesus could recalibrate his thinking through this amazing encounter with the other, maybe the same is possible for those of us who believe him to be a distinctive, even singular revelation of the divine. The gospel surprise here is that the stranger is not only worthy of our hospitality and mission, but, in this reverse gospel, the stranger can actually be a *source* of grace and ministry to us. Such seems possible, however, only if we are willing to engage in the promising paradox of believing from the outside-in.

2

The Power of Language

A theologian is someone who watches their language in the presence of God.

—*Gerald O'Collins (Lash, 2011)*

One of the more celebrated twentieth-century quotes about language was penned by the English author Virginia Woolf (d. 1941). In her novel, *Jacob's Room*, one of her characters announced, "Language is wine upon the lips" (Woolf 1922, 40). That vivid image effectively captures something of the intoxicating potential of language to move us, comfort us, and even seduce us. Evidence that Woolf touched something of the power of speech in this modern proverb comes not only from the empirical data that her quote consistently appears in innumerable books and online resources of quotations, but also from the cultural evidence as it frequently adorns T-shirts, coffee mugs, and even mouse pads in the modern marketplace.

There is, however, a dark side to Woolf's quote, something that may be obscured by the mugs and mouse pads. Yet it is important to consider this dark side when confronting some of the challenges of language, especially as they relate to belief sharing. In point of fact, wine on the lips is not always a desirable guest. To a teetotaler, any alcoholic beverage is certainly an unwelcome intruder, shattering one's commitment to abstinence for whatever religious, philosophical, or other reasons it was undertaken. Beyond teetotalers, wine on the lips can be more than an unwelcome visitor for an alcoholic: it can literally be a type of poison with the potential to derail completely one's well-being. I am frequently reminded of that threat by a good-humored friend who is a recovering alcoholic. When asked at a recent St. Patrick's Day party if he wanted some green beer, in typical fashion he quipped, "No thank you, I have to be somewhere before Christmas!"

Language can similarly be an unwelcome intruder or even a toxic ingredient with the potential to derail or even poison a conversation. The issue of whether language is a gift or a threat is particularly tricky when it involves the sharing of deep beliefs or spiritual convictions. We previously admitted that language often makes demands on our conversation partners and that any reimagined form of theological reflection is probably not possible without exacting some toll. At the same time, the toll that is required through our use of language should not be so burdensome that it disables such a conversation not only from getting started but actually from moving forward.

In this chapter we will consider a few key aspects of language and dialogue important for effective and respectful reinventions of theological reflection. These will start with a consideration of the different linguistic cautions that confront theologians and those that are part of any inter-belief dialogue. We will then turn to the philosopher Ludwig Wittgenstein and consider his contribution through the frame of language games. This will lead us to consider reflective believing more in terms of verbs rather than nouns. Finally, we will attend to the various types of "languages" that might be both suitable and beneficial for engaging in reflective believing. Storytelling will receive particular attention here.

WATCHING OUR LANGUAGE BEFORE WHOM?

It was the British Roman Catholic theologian Nicholas Lash who turned public attention to the quotation by Gerald O'Collins cited at the outset of this chapter. Lash recalled the quotation almost forty years after hearing it in a seminar that O'Collins, an Australian Jesuit, was teaching. At the time that Lash publicly related this memory, he was a celebrated theologian in his own right: a professor of divinity at Cambridge who, at the moment, was receiving an honorary degree from Durham University. His citation of O'Collins's definition of a theologian was part of a speech at Durham in which Lash argued that academic theologians shared many things in common with university researchers in other fields (e.g., a passion for accuracy and truthfulness, a sense of collaboration and a lively imagination) (Lash 2011).

The language of university researchers—including theologians—can often be highly technical while still remaining quite imaginative. Its imaginative aspect is the proposing of claims or hypotheses that subsequently must undergo rigorous examination and testing, whether that occurs in a scientific laboratory or through discussion with other experts in the field. Precision and accuracy in the testing and the reporting of this testing are vital for establishing the credibility of any hypothesis. Advances in medicine, for example, rely upon accurate scientific search for the development of increasingly effective therapies and treatments. When data is falsified—as alleged in the case of Dr. Potti of Duke Universit, who studied the gene patterns in various forms of cancer (*Economist* 2011)—physicians are misled and patients potentially harmed through ineffective or even dangerous therapies.

Similarly, when professional theologians assert as true what is questionable or even falsified, believers can be misled and even harmed. A notable example of this was a presentation by Professor Karen King of Harvard Divinity School at an international meeting of Coptic scholars in Rome on September 18, 2012. In that presentation, Professor King announced the existence of a papyrus fragment, which on the surface could indicate that Jesus was married; she even called the fragment "The Gospel of Jesus' Wife." While carbon dating tests and other scientific studies of the ink and papyrus have never been made public, it is widely believed that the papyrus is a forgery constructed out of material borrowed from the Coptic Gospel of Thomas (Bernhard 2012). Even the *Harvard Theological Review*, the prestigious journal from her home institution that had accepted Professor King's work for publication, decided to postpone publishing her findings in the wake of such criticism. While there is no evidence that Professor King was involved in what appears to be a forgery or ever believed that the fragment in some way proved that Jesus was actually married, her presentation at that conference in one of the most celebrated cities of Christianity ignited a firestorm of responses from Christian leaders around the globe. These leaders believed that, for the good of their followers and the historic Christianity they represented, they needed to protect and defend the traditional teaching that Jesus was unmarried.

Because of their responsibility not only to reflect upon their personal beliefs but also to guide, enhance, and correct the beliefs of others, theologians have a particular responsibility to be rigorous and accurate in their language. Thus, O'Collins's quote about watching his language in the presence of some transcendent seems appropriately weighty. Furthermore, since beliefs are usually ascribed both to individuals and, more frequently, to communities, the leaders of such communities take the safeguarding of those beliefs and the language used to express them very seriously. Those whom leaders deem gifted and inspirational for expressing central beliefs are often literally or figuratively canonized. Those who push any doctrine beyond the realm of what is judged acceptable or orthodox are alternately sanctioned, defrocked, excommunicated, or otherwise shunned.

While theologians or academics who speak about religious or spiritual issues have a professional responsibility to watch their language in the presence of whatever transcendent they honor—be that God or their academic guild—ministers and other believers involved in reflective believing and dialogue around such reflection have a somewhat different responsibility. Without trying to dichotomize these into two completely different forms of speech, I would suggest that instead of *watching our language in the presence of God*, reflective believing puts more stress on *watching our language in the presence of each other*, especially the "stranger." While some might consider the shared act of reflective believing mostly about objective truth telling or an exercise in apologetics intended to defend their own beliefs, for me belief sharing is more about meaning making in the hopes of finding at least mutual respect, if not common ground, with people of diverse beliefs. Thus, it is less about public debate than about reverent engagement. That is why this reimagined form of theological reflection needs to balance accuracy with accommodation in ways professional theologians may not always be obliged or even inclined to do. This seems appropriate if you conceive of reflective believing as an exercise less intent on proving some dogmatic point and more about forging a life-giving interpretation that has at least respectability, if not currency, across multiple belief systems.

WITTGENSTEIN AND LANGUAGE GAMES

A voice that might help us grasp more effectively some of the differences between theological inquiry and reflective believing—two distinctive, yet not unrelated, forms of discourse—is that of the Austrian-British philosopher Ludwig Wittgenstein (d. 1951). Wittgenstein introduced the concept of a "language game" in his influential *Philosophical Investigations* (2009). Initially, the sound of that phrase could be off-putting, as it might suggest that the goal of any such game is to trick another through a clever, yet deceptive, use of words. Wittgenstein is not concerned about how words can deceive, however, but how language (like any game) has certain rules and procedures. For example, he speaks about the game of chess (Wittgenstein 2009, no. 31). Wittgenstein observes that just showing a chess piece to someone and saying "this is a king" or "this is a knight" does not mean that an individual now understands how to play this ancient game. Anyone, of course, could make up her own rules and play a game with the chess pieces in the same way, for example, that she plays checkers. It might be an enjoyable game, but it is clearly not chess. Having the name or language for something does not ensure that someone will speak appropriately or communicate effectively. Wittgenstein concludes that naming in itself is neither a complete nor a sufficient way of knowing, and a more authentic mode of apprehension requires a set of rules or some kind of grammar to move the game along.

Wittgenstein further recognizes that within the same broadly spoken language—whether that be Hindi or Spanish—many different kinds of language games are possible. Giving orders is different from making a joke, and reporting an event is different from praying. The number of such games within a given language is innumerable, and new ones come into existence all the time. One contemporary example of the latter is tweeting, a compact form of social communication unknown before 2006. While new language games emerge, others become obsolete and are eventually forgotten (Wittgenstein 2009, no. 23).

Wittgenstein helps me understand with particular clarity that theological speculation and belief sharing can be understood as different language games with different rules. While bearing some family resemblance, like chess and checkers, they are more like cousins than siblings and cannot always be played the same way. One of the many challenges facing beginning divinity students, seminarians, and others studying chaplaincy or spiritual leadership is that they are often required to learn two new language games simultaneously (e.g., systematic theology and theological reflection). This challenge is amplified in some contexts that unnecessarily emphasize the dissimilarity of these forms of discourse—for example, separating systematic or biblical studies into departments celebrated for their rigor and gravitas, while relegating courses in pastoral care or worship into ministry divisions that lack such esteem.

Individually, each of these genres is challenging enough in its own right. To paraphrase Wittgenstein, just because one can use terms like *enlightenment* or *grace* or *revelation* does not mean that someone is speaking much less thinking systematically. Similarly, simply using language about beliefs or values or, conversely, listening intently while someone else does the same does not mean that one has successfully negotiated the admittedly porous boundaries between systematic theology and theological reflection. This threshold crossing is further complicated by Wittgenstein's reminder that some language games disappear and new games emerge. Thus, even if one knew how to "play" theological reflection à la Whiteheads last year, that does not mean that those rules transfer into our current context and the manner in which the theological reflection "game" needs to be played today.

REFLECTIVE BELIEVING

The phrase "reflective believing" is my attempt to name the new language game that I perceive is emerging out of the previous language game we called theological reflection. By doing so I am not suggesting that theological reflection is some obsolete enterprise that needs to be abandoned. Many will continue to use the language and classical methods of theological reflection to great benefit. In this chaordic context of such great diversity in ways of believing, however, the term itself as well as the rules for playing the game of theological reflection seem increasingly limited. For example, theology is not a shared framework across belief systems and certainly not a preferred term for Sikhs or Jains. Muslim scholars also have difficulty with the term, and some believe that theology is not the way to spiritual knowledge. Reza Shah-Kazemi contends that "theology is almost like a veil obscuring this knowledge and a barrier against it" (Shah-Kazemi 2010, 95). The language of interfaith certainly has currency in this chaordic context, and there is much talk of "interfaith dialogue," and some even suggest the possibility of interfaith reflection (Thompson 2008, 171–74). "Faith," however, is not a shared category across belief systems and, for example, neither humanists nor Buddhists technically have a "faith." Furthermore, while interfaith dialogue can be concerned with the task of meaning making that is at the core of reflective believing, it also can have very different political or social purposes (e.g., lowering tensions between religious communities, or confronting the prejudice that religious minorities so often face).

I would contend, however, that no matter how one positions themselves around the issue of religion, everyone has beliefs or—as we will further discuss—engages in a process of believing. As a Roman Catholic, when I go to Mass on Sunday, I join with others in saying "I believe in God." Similarly, atheist Chris Stedman talks about his "beliefs" (2012, 102), as does the Dalai Lama (Gyatso 2005). While our ways of believing are vastly different, it seems that the language of believing provides broader common ground than that of traditional forms of Christian theology or even what the Abrahamic faiths hold in common, and more adequately names a process upon which all of us may reflect if we wish.

IMAGINATION

One way that may be helpful in clarifying this emerging language game of reflective believing and distinguish (without divorcing) it from the language game of theological inquiry is by examining the different roles that imagination assumes in each of these processes. Nicholas Lash's previously cited ideas help me both admit and applaud the role of imagination in the work of academics such as professional theologians. Trying to imagine the nature of Allah, or the essence of the covenant between God and the chosen people, or the power of the Holy Spirit for communities of believers is daunting. Often, professional theologians write scholarly articles or books, which are sophisticated attempts to prove certain hypotheses born of their highly enriched imaginations. The testing of such hypotheses comes in the discourse, the reviews, and the seminars in which they are debated, and either the raft of invitations that follows their publication or the professional shunning that could also ensue. While such hypotheses seldom can be empirically proven, as is possible in some of the hard sciences, they can find increasing acceptance until they are commonly recognized as true or at least plausible.

Reflective believing (or RB) is a different language game than theological inquiry. One of the differences is that in RB there is little if any proving. There might be some "testing" to the extent that those of us who witness the belief-disclosing of another might test out some of those ways of believing in our own lives. What seems especially distinctive from the work of systematic theological inquiry, however, is that the work of reflective believing usually does not begin with an imaginative hypothesis. Rather, it often starts with personal or communal experiences that are subsequently narrated by individuals in the hopes of discerning some meaning from those experiences. It is this attempt to make sense out of one's experience—both for the narrator and for those listening to that reflection—that is the more imaginative act and seems to require the more inquisitive stance of the seeker rather than the critical stance of the theologian. Rather than a "Wow, that's wrong (or odd or stupid)" evaluation of another's thinking, RB is more an invitation to awe with just enough parallel anxiety that at least momentarily makes us wonder—like the characters in Chaim Potok's *The Book of Lights* (see textbox 2.1)—"What are we all about?" The different role and even placement of the imaginative process (e.g., often an originating move for the scholar, but as more of a responsive move for reflective believing) helps to clarify further for me how and why RB can be considered a distinctive language game.

In some ways, at its core, this book could be considered a language game exploration. Through dialogue with multiple individuals and groups as well as by reflecting upon and sometimes rethinking my own experiences, I am trying to discern how the rules are shifting as the game modulates (1) from systematic theology to theological reflection, (2) from theological reflection to interfaith dialogue, (3) from interfaith dialogue to interfaith theological reflection, and (4) finally to the emerging process of reflective believing. One distinguishing rule of reflective believing that has become clear to me in this

---

TEXTBOX 2.1

In Chaim Potok's novel *The Book of Lights*, a young rabbi from Brooklyn travels to Japan from Korea during the Korean War. One afternoon he stands with a Jewish friend before what is either a Shinto shrine or a Buddhist shrine. They watch a man stand before the altar, with his eyes closed and his hands pressed together in what a Jew might consider "prayer." The young rabbi turns to his friend and asks:

"Do you think our God is listening to him, John?"

"I don't know, chappy. I never thought of it. "

"Neither did I until now. If he's not listening, why not? If he is listening, then—well, what are we all about John?" (Potok 1981, 248)

process is the previously noted idea that RB is more about watching one's language in the presence of others than in the presence of some transcendent. A litmus test that this rule is being observed is the reluctance by anyone who engages in this newly emerging game to critique or correct the way another believes. Instead, it should nurture a sense of wonder at the range and depths of another's believing.

IN PRAISE OF GERUNDS AND VERBS

In the process of exploring this topic, I have had the privilege of consulting with a wide range of people across an amazing spectrum of beliefs. In one of those conversations, a Buddhist teacher raised valuable cautions about employing the language of "belief" in any reimagined form of theological reflection. She clarified her concern by noting that—from the perspective of her tradition—self-emptying was an important process on the path to mindfulness and enlightenment. She was concerned, however, that speaking about "beliefs" could give the impression that these were a kind of possession to which one might cling, as Christians might cling to certain doctrines about Christ that they were unwilling to give up, even for the sake of interfaith collaboration. While I do believe it is possible, and even necessary, to treasure my own religious or spiritual convictions in the midst of such dialogue, I still appreciated her concern about what might be considered the inert and even obstinate nature of nouns.

In the previous chapter we borrowed the image of liquidity from the Polish sociologist Zygmunt Bauman, who contrasted the dynamic nature of liquids with the more inanimate nature of solids. Zygmunt believes that—both in thought and in practice—contemporary global flows are characterized by a marked liquidity in contrast to previous eras, which he perceives as less dynamic and more stolid. We proposed that liquidity is an apt characterization of the way that a growing number of individuals situate themselves around issues of spirituality and religion today. The increasing number of adults in the United States, especially those under thirty years of age, who identify themselves as believers but unaffiliated, or spiritual but not religious, symbolizes something of the paradoxical fluidity that defines contemporary believing in my own context.

Effectively engaging in dialogue around issues of religion or spirituality in this liquid moment requires a style of discourse that is as fluid as the environment in which it occurs. My own language of "reflective believing" rather than "theological reflection" or "interfaith reflection" is an attempt to explore and model such dynamism. Thinking in *nouns* (e.g., "reflection") could be metaphorically akin to sitting still. Any form of theological reflection that functions as some exchange of prepackaged beliefs that must be safeguarded at any cost is analogous to each of us erecting our own tollbooths in the center lane of what is supposed to be a conversational expressway. Traffic is certainly not going to flow very easily over such a terrain.

Verbs and "action nouns" (also called gerunds) embody more satisfactorily the ebb and flow that marks any true journey into ourselves as well as the graced and precarious journey into the mystery of the other. My good friend Herbert Anderson well capitalizes on this instinct in his coauthoring of five books on the process of being married. He aptly titled them *Leaving Home*, *Becoming Married*, *Regarding Children*, *Promising Again*, and *Living Alone*. The titles—as well as their sequence—alert the reader to the authors' presuppositions that marriage is an extended and eventful journey, a verb and not a noun, often as unpredictable as waves on a beach.

While professional theologians often play their language games with well-defined and concrete goals such as positing truths, establishing orthodoxy, or reinterpreting doctrines, the language game of reflective believing tends to be more tentative and exploratory. The Whiteheads captured something of this spirit early in their method. The first and essential step in their process of theological reflection is not discerning or judging or defending some concept or belief, but rather what they called *attending*. They described this move as one that begins in active patience and requires holding oneself still enough to hear. They contend that such a venture requires a receptive though not passive stance and its litmus test is the ability to respond with accuracy and empathy (Whitehead and Whitehead 1995, 69).

There are many positives to considering *attending* as a first move in the exploration we are calling reflective believing. In the context of our current discussion about language, the "action noun" *attending* is particularly potent for its capacity to keep us oriented toward the present moment. Reflective believing—like any authentic form of theological reflection—is a venture into the now. It is true that the process often involves recalling past experiences (e.g., a ministerial encounter) that spark the reflecting and then putting those experiences in dialogue with some aspect of your religious heritage (e.g., sacred writings) or personal canon (e.g., an influential poem or piece of music) in the process of meaning making. At the same time, at its core, RB cannot be about excavating some hermetically sealed "evidence" or experience from the past, plopping that data on the floor in front of someone whose experiences or believing is different than our own, in order to prove some point in the present (e.g., about "their error"). Whenever we do such excavating as truth-proving, we not only metaphorically erect some tollbooth in the conversation but potentially construct an entire toll plaza that can shut down all dialogue. A classic example from my own tradition is that potent conversation stopper: "Scripture has always taught that _____ (fill in the blank)."

Since reflective believing is not about delivering a previously cooked position but engaging in the lively act of reflecting for the sake of meaning making, gerunds like *attending* (in all of its auditory resonance) better capture the vibrancy and immediacy of this evolving language game. This acoustic art is very different from the plastic arts such as painting, since, when Rembrandt or Picasso were finished applying the oils or pastels, the painting continued to exist, sometimes for centuries. Unlike paint or glass or stone, sound cannot be physically captured in icon, window, or sculpture. Yes, sounds can be digitally sampled and retrieved, but an iPod or CD is not the material of music in the same way that a stone can literally become the material of a sculpture. The irrepressible composer and music director Alice Parker continuously reminded every member of any vocal ensemble she directed that music is not a constellation of marks on a page. That's notation! Rather than dots and squiggles on a printed staff, music is a verb—an organized *sounding*. When the sound waves are no longer emanating from sitar or saxophone, baritone, or bassoon then the music is over, even though a musical score might remain. As the philosopher Susanne Langer understood, sounds like music "spread out time for our direct and complete apprehension . . . [music] makes time audible!" (1953, 110). Music from an orchestra or in the lyricism of the stranger's voice is an encounter with the virtual now.

Reflective believing is more like music making than painting. It is an intentional belief-gesture that requires entering into the present moment and a willingness to remain immersed in the dynamic now. And while there are some aspects of this reimagined form of theological reflection that can be accomplished individually, like most forms of traditional dancing in the West, reflective believing ordinarily takes at least "two to tango." Furthermore, this particular tango form is not a thoroughly choreographed dance in which each move is mapped, rehearsed, and polished for the performance. No, this is more improvised dancing. Contrary to popular opinion, improvisation is not simply making something up on the spur of the moment. Rather, it is disciplined preparation for a reinvention in the present, for the making of music or dance or comedy never seen before, and by definition unrepeatable in the future. Comedians and jazz musicians, actors and organists, all study and practice improvisation. Similarly, any expedition into reflective believing is enhanced by disciplined preparation. The goal of such preparation is to keep us vital and attuned in the process of attending and speaking. A basic rule of comedic improvisation—similar to playing in a finely tuned jazz quartet—is the need to respect what others give you: to listen intently to their words or music and allow their lead to take you where you have never been before. Such respectful attending can create an opening for a refreshed present marked by revitalized believing and respect. The language game of RB, like every language game Wittgenstein imagined, is an action—a verb—in which the very act of speaking is not only a linguistic exercise but also "a form of life" (Wittgenstein 2009, no. 23).

GAMING BEYOND WORDS

Reflective believing as a reimagined form of theological reflection is proposed here as a new form of gaming with its own set of distinctive rules and strategies. One of those rules for this new species of language game is that it can and does happen through a variety of linguistic forms as diverse as storytelling and poetry. That does not mean, however, that it can only occur through language narrowly conceived. Spoken words structured according to a grammar of respect and wonder are certainly one ordinary and probably even necessary form of speech for birthing this new language game. There are, however, many other types of utterances that may be not only useful but also important in nourishing this unique form of discourse. We will consider a few of these.

Silence

A former music teacher of mine used to say that without the rests, music would simply be noise. Pauses between the sounds can, in their own way, be just as powerful as the sounds themselves. Much of the strength and drama in the first four bars of Beethoven's astounding Fifth Symphony, for example, would evaporate without the rests that set apart those two opening sets of descending minor thirds (see figure 2.1). In the same way, pauses in speech

FIGURE 2.1.

can make the difference between a good presentation and rhetoric indelibly etched in the memory. Visit YouTube.com, for example, and replay Martin Luther King Jr.'s timeless 1963 speech from the Lincoln memorial, punctuated by the reoccurring phrase, "I have a dream." The speech is rendered all the more memorable by its dramatic and insistent pauses.

In a similar way, sometimes our best move in the language game of reflective believing is choosing silence. Like a student hospital chaplain on our first day of visiting patients, we often have the urge to fill every moment following a difficult story or heartfelt witness with chatter. It is a common instinct but seldom a necessary one and not always even a useful one. Being invited to journey into another's way of believing is an invitation to holy ground. In this era of increased diversity around such believing, another's holy ground can be a quite foreign space for us. We are stretched in this experience to feel empathy—maybe best described as "my heart in your chest." Educators Grant Wiggins and Jay McTighe believe that empathy is an important form of insight, and that even in public education it is essential that we design courses and curricula that lead to this capacity. They consider it a form of insight because, in their words, "It involves the ability to get beyond the odd, alien, seemingly weird opinions or people to find what is meaningful in them" (Wiggins and McTighe 2005, 99). Thus they believe that true education from this empathetic perspective involves not only some "intellectual change of mind but a significant change of heart" (99).

Given today's chaordic context, maybe empathy itself has to be reimagined. That seems to be the view of David Augsburger (1986, 31), who coined the term *interpathy* as a way to underscore how empathy needs to be transformed as it moves across contexts and cultures. A Roman Catholic journeying into the belief circle of an agnostic, a Hindu hearing the conversion story of a conservative Jew, an evangelical Christian pondering the reverence Muslims show for the Qur'an: these are moves across contexts and cultures, and maybe even universes and galaxies. On the way to interpathy, sometimes silence is the most respectful and intelligent choice we can make.

Body Language

Besides speaking or choosing silence, there are other "languages" that may be helpful in the process of reflective believing. Since the breakthrough work of social scientists such as Albert Mehrabian and Susan Ferris in the mid-twentieth century, it is widely accepted that we speak not only with our mouths but also with our eyes and hands and the rest of our bodies as well. While social scientists differ on how much of our communication is actually nonverbal—opinions commonly range from 50 percent up to 80 percent—virtually no social scientist discounts the power of body language in human communication.

Attempting to prescribe principles or even guidelines for the nonverbal aspects of belief sharing could verge on the foolhardy, since every form of embodied speech is a highly contextualized event. In some contexts, for example, looking directly into the eyes of the speaker or the listener can be most appropriate and even expected, whereas in other contexts it can be perceived as not only impolite but also insolent. This is an awareness it took me years to appreciate in teaching students from other cultures and contexts, some of whom refused to look directly at me when I was speaking to them. I thought they were showing disinterest in what I was saying. Eventually they helped me understand that they were actually honoring me as their teacher and elder, though I never thought of myself as either distinguished or old. Maybe it is enough to say that whatever nonverbal communication we employ, it needs to enhance the quality of attending, communicate reverence for the other, and nourish the gift of interpathy between those daring enough to disclose their beliefs and those sufficient respectfully to journey with them.

Ritualizing

A sometimes overlooked "language" of reflective believing that also needs to be considered here is that of ritualizing. This is admittedly a broad and somewhat ambiguous term, and maybe its own language game. Such ambiguity is magnified by the fact that ritualizing activity is not confined to humans, as entomologists and zoologists describe in some detail how insects and animals ritualize as part of their own cycles of hunting, mating, birthing, and dying. Human beings also ritualize, sometimes for the same reasons as other species. What is unique to humans, however, is symbolizing and ritualizing as a way of believing. Ritualizing as an aspirational act—a way of expressing admittedly inexplicable hopes and dreams, frequently in the face of some crisis—has characterized humanity from whatever its foggy origins. Sometimes this aspirational aspect of ritualizing has revealed itself in the ways that ancient humanoids (as early as 25,000 BCE) have buried their dead with food, weapons, and other aids for the mysterious journey into the other side of life. Other times it expressed itself well before the birth of writing through the shaping of megalithic stones orientated for greeting the spring equinox or marking the darkest night of the year. Theistic religions since at least the Bronze Age have shaped their ritualizing as acts of worship and allegiance to multiple or individual supreme beings from whom they alternately expect deliverance or prosperity, while others on a path to enlightenment ritualize in order to discipline the body and enhance mindfulness.

Contemporary ritual theories have critiqued the more traditional view of ritual as a vehicle for delivering content or a way to impose beliefs. Rather than a delivery system for doctrines or "nouns," ritualizing is better understood as a dynamic strategy—some even say a "technology"—a collective of verbs for negotiating relationships more than delivering belief (Foley 2012). From this more tactical perspective, traditional religious rituals can be understood not so much as events that clarify who the gods are or how one travels safely into the underworld, as much as methods for designating who actually gets to define the gods, personally undertake, or even more broadly control travel into the underworld. More often than not these gatekeepers are elderly, privileged, and sometimes celibate males from the dominant tribe. Akin to the role of magic in J. K. Rowling's inspiring Harry Potter books, ritual has the power to be oppressive and exclusionary (as in the hands of Malfoy, Voldemort, and their conspirators), or, alternatively, it can be liberating and inclusive (as wielded by Harry, Hermione, and Ron along with their families and friends).

Reconceiving ritualizing as a path rather than as content guides our understanding about its potential as a language for reflective believing. Engaging in a ritual that opens the path of another's believing—such as yoga practice or a tea ceremony—can be a rich and rewarding strategy in the language game we are calling reflective believing. For the beginner in this journey, the path of another's ritualizing first calls us to openness and empathy in attending to the ritual, assuming a stance of receptiveness to whatever stimuli it impresses on our senses. As we grow more accustomed to entering the ritualizing of others, moving deeper into reflective believing in this mode could be an invitation to transition from what anthropologists label "observing" toward the more affirming stance of "participating." While attentive observing is certainly its own form of participation, migrating toward "participating" ordinarily involves engaging in the gestures, vocalizations, or other actions that define the ritualizing. Our level of attentive participation needs to respect both our own capacity to engage and the capacity of the ritual and its leaders to allow our participation.

Claire Wolfteich is a Roman Catholic theologian who teaches practical theology at Boston University. Claire has documented her experience with her Christian students as they attended Sabbath worship at orthodox, conservative, and reform synagogues. In some of those ritual events the Christians (Claire included) were invited to be observers while Jews offered prayer. In other situations, the Christian guests were invited to be more active participants. In her reflections on that journey, Claire emphasizes not only how important it is to study Sabbath practice but also how critical it is for future Christian leaders to *experience* Sabbath in their journey toward personal transformation (Wolfteich 2011, 268). Practice, in this case the practice of ritualizing, is its own form of knowing that cannot be replaced by other (e.g., text centered) forms of knowing.

Entering into another's ritual life or inviting them into our own is not about ritual tourism or becoming a cultural voyeur. Rather, it is journeying into the mystical through symbols and silence. One of the more dramatic examples of such ritualizing that could be understood as a form of reflective believing is practiced by members of the Monastic Interreligious Dialogue. Founded in the 1970s by Roman Catholic monks, it initiated a program of "spiritual exchanges" between Christian monks of the West and monastics of various religions from the East. One of the more evocative forms of such spiritual exchange has been the sharing in the daily monastic life of another religious tradition over a period of weeks and even months. Buddhist and Christian monks have consistently engaged in this form of dialogue, a practice praised by both the Dalai Lama and Pope John Paul II (Bereza 2004). There are even situations in which such spiritual exchange becomes a way of sustaining community life. Few are as striking as the interfaith ashram established by the Roman Catholic priest John Dupuche with another priest who identifies with the Camaldolese tradition. Together they established an interfaith household in Melbourne, Australia, that also serves as the "parish house" for the local Catholic church. In residence in this Roman Catholic "rectory" are also Swami Sannyasanand, a yogi of the Satyananda lineage, and Venerable Lobsang Tendar, a Tibetan Buddhist monk of the Gyuto tradition (Dupuche 2013).

I admit that as a Roman Catholic who has taught worship for decades, the language of ritualization is attractive to me. At the same time, I am acutely aware that ritualizing, in its multitude of forms, is a constant across all human societies. It is a particularly valuable strategy in the believing process, be that for theists or nontheists. Concerning the latter, I am struck by the extraordinary amount of space that Alain de Botton devotes to writing about ritual in his *Religion for Atheists*—a self-proclaimed "Non-Believer's Guide to the Uses of Religion." His second chapter on "community," for example, dedicates nine pages to extolling the benefits of the "Catholic Mass" (2012, 30–39). Similarly, he generously allocates multiple pages to Jewish rituals of atonement, grieving, and bar mitzvahs (de Botton 2012, 52–68). He then argues that secularists should establish parallel rituals—devoid of theistic overtones. De Botton is concerned about building community, nurturing virtues such as kindness and tenderness, and reshaping education so that it produces moral (and not just market-savvy) individuals. He instinctively and philosophically understands that rituals are a "technology" that can be employed by theists and nontheists, believers of every stripe, to achieve such noble goals.

Storytelling

Besides silence, body language, and ritualizing, there is a final mode of sharing that is especially effective in the language game we are calling reflective believing: that of storytelling. I first began exploring the power of stories when teaching a seminar with Herbert Anderson on worship and pastoral care. Over the years of that seminar I began to appreciate not only how ubiquitous was the practice of storytelling but also what an amazing gift it was for connecting the diversity of women and men, lay and clerical, from widely varying faith traditions, cultures, and contexts who shared in those seminars. Some of our common learning from that experience were brought together in our book *Mighty Stories, Dangerous Rituals* (see textbox 2.2).

Since that writing I have often thought about how various belief traditions have honored the process of storytelling. One of the ways they have done so is not only by telling stories about their gods but also by presuming that the gods

TEXTBOX 2.2

"In the aftermath of the massacres that occurred in Rwanda in the early 1990's, a woman psychologist was asked to visit one of the many refugee camps of Rwandans in Tanzania. It seems that the women of that camp, though safe from the slaughter, were not sleeping. During her visit to the refugees, the psychologist learned that the women, who had witnessed the murder of family and friends, had been told not to speak of such atrocities in the camp. The women followed this instruction, but the memories of the carnage haunted them, and they could not sleep. The psychologist decided that in response to this situation she would set up a story tree: a safe place for the women to speak of their experiences. Every morning she went out to the edge of the camp and waited under the canopy of a huge shade tree. The first day no one came. On the second day one woman appeared, told her story, and left. Another showed up the following day, then another and another. Within the span of a few days, hundreds of women were gathering under the tree each morning to listen and to share their tales of loss, fear, and death. Finally, after weeks of listening, the psychologist knew that the story tree was working. Reports confirmed that the women in the camp were now sleeping. The only difficulty was that the psychologist wasn't." (Anderson and Foley 1997, 3)

themselves were storytellers. Many religious traditions—like that of the ancient Greeks—taught that the gods engaged in powerful actions before humans existed. In Greek mythology, for example, there is the founding story of how Zeus was hidden by his mother so that his father would not destroy him, and how he subsequently grew to be king of the gods. Although no human beings were present for many of these events, we still have stories about them. One can only conclude that the gods themselves were storytellers and that they were the sources of our narratives about them. From a Jewish perspective, Elie Wiesel muses in his *The Gates of the Forest* that God made people because God loves stories (1966, Prologue). In a similar vein, both Buddha and Jesus are remembered by their respective traditions as being gifted storytellers.

Besides this ancient connection of storytelling to celebrated traditions of believing, there are other key reasons why this is such an effective strategy in the language game we are calling RB. An obvious but sometimes overlooked one is that everyone has a story. We might not always think that our story is unique or utterly interesting to anyone else, and we might not even consider our own personal narrative of much value. Nonetheless, we all have one and often invoke story-snippets in the ordinary give and take of daily life. How many times have we told someone where we grew up, or how we moved to the city we now call home, or where we went to school? Each of these is a story-snippet culled from the more comprehensive narrative that comprises our unique autobiography. Virtually every time we introduce ourselves to a stranger or to a group, at a block party or at our first day at a new job, we end up telling something of our story.

Not only does each of us have a unique story, but it is commonly recognized that human beings frequently and consistently think in narratives. Beyond telling stories, in many ways we find it both easy and useful to perceive life itself as an unfolding story, whether that be a tragedy, a comedy, or something in between. Narrative is actually a quite useful tool for collecting data and connecting the dots. I was riding with a friend in his car a few years ago when someone in another vehicle ran a red light, hit the car in front of us, and forced us to swerve up onto a curb. When the police arrived, they basically asked everyone involved to "tell the tale" of what happened. The final police report was, in many respects, an official "short story" that wove together the information about the three drivers, their cars, and that particular intersection into a comprehensive unit.

While storytelling often relates data such as the material contained in that police novella, storytelling is decidedly not the same as reporting. Reporting purportedly has the purpose of outlining information in as dispassionate and objective a manner as possible. Storytelling, on the other hand, is intensely personal and fundamentally an act of interpretation. My guess is that the police officers collecting information heard differing narrations of that event from the many people involved in or witnessing the accident. That is not because anyone was necessarily being dishonest, but rather because people had different experiences of the accident, were standing or sitting in different locations, were more or less involved in the accident, and thus interpreted those experiences through the stories they told from the social geography they occupied at that moment.

Storytelling is one of the most common forms of meaning making that humans employ. From an early age we tell stories to explain to our parents how the vase got broken, why our teacher gave us a bad grade, and why we had a fight with our best friend. While on the surface a story may appear to be a form of explaining a series of events, it is also a way of making sense of the world and our place in it. A sophisticated example of such meaning making is the memoir, such as the excruciatingly funny and terribly poignant *Running with Scissors* in which Augusten Burroughs narrates how he came to survive and even flourish under the most extraordinary of circumstances. A friend who published a quite revealing autobiography once told me that he wrote the work not to critique others but because he needed to do it for his own well-being and to make a honest accounting of himself. In a similar vein, sharing stories of our journey into believing is not simply reporting some spiritual pilgrimage but is a way to make sense of that believing—not only for those listening to this tale but also, and maybe even especially, for ourselves in the telling.

Our storytelling is very personal, both because it is about us and because it makes public some of the ways we try to make sense of life. Consequently, it can often be an invitation to profound intimacy. I am constantly surprised by how much detail about the most secret parts of one's life certain interviewers can coax out of people for broadcast on television or the Internet. It suggests that we really do want to tell our story. For that to happen, however, we need the presence of a sympathetic soul who can willingly enter our world without judging us more harshly than we judge ourselves. Authentic storytelling is an invitation to respectful and empathetic story listening and a distinctive form of mutuality.

Inviting someone to listen to our belief-journey could, therefore, be considered an invitation into a kind of spiritual communion. It is not necessarily a communion of agreement, in which the listening implies some implicit consent or affirmation about the believing that unfolds in the telling. Rather, it is a communion of respect, of interpathy, even of awe in the presence of another's belief-narrative. Accepting such an invitation requires great discipline that enables us to inquire without disparaging, to respond without judging, and to witness without necessarily agreeing.

This invitation to intimacy as spiritual community may be one of the more distinguishing facets of reflective believing, especially in differentiating it from more traditional forms of theological inquiry and even interfaith dialogue. While there are probably no pure forms of any of these language games, the one we are calling RB is more a heart game than a head game. While it can contribute to problem solving and other more practical pursuits, it fundamentally is an act of care that helps create an atmosphere of respect especially in view of the ever-shifting patterns of believing that mark the current age and even our own lives.

3

Goal Setting for Reflective Believing

What you get by achieving your goals is not as important as what you become by achieving your goals.

—attributed to Henry David Thoreau

Among the new academic disciplines that developed in the scientific boom at the end of the twentieth century was one called "futurology," now more commonly known as "future studies." This discipline—which some consider a science, while others think of it more as an art—has varying and sometimes quite different goals. For example, some in this field prefer an approach intent on *predicting* future directions in technology or human development, while others are inclined to a more applied form that is concerned with actually trying to *create* the future. The predictive form of futurology is apt to expend considerable energy studying trends and probabilities, while mindful to calculate for the unexpected that is always in our future, in the hopes of developing a credible forecast about some aspect of our future. Thus, for example, in attempting to project whether there might be an impending food shortage in some part of the globe, agencies like the World Food Programme at the United Nations study population growth as well as the means people employ for acquiring or producing food in a given area. At the same time such calculations need to take into account virtually unpredictable variables, such as climate changes or social unrest, which can significantly impact the availability of food.

The more applied approach in futurology is less about predicting a future than creating one. In this approach the focus is on some preferred objective or outcome that requires a kind of working backward from that goal, calculating all of the steps necessary to get to that destination and then correctly executing each of those steps, one after the other. One of the more celebrated examples of this applied form of futurology in US history was the Apollo 11 mission in 1969 that put the first humans on the moon. It was President John F. Kennedy, before a joint session of Congress in 1961, who announced the ambitious goal of sending astronauts to the moon by the end of that decade. In order to accomplish such an extraordinary feat, the National Aeronautics and Space Administration (NASA) had first to chart all of the steps to get to the moon, and then achieve success in literally tens of thousands of these operations and experiments as it inched toward that goal. This required not only designing and testing the rockets, space suits, lunar module, and every other piece of equipment needed for that task, but also staging almost one hundred major launches and attempted launches of moon probes and orbiters, manned and unmanned, from Mercury to Gemini to Apollo programs until that "giant step" of 1969.

The reimagined form of theological reflection we are calling reflective believing is certainly more art than science and does not require input from a mega-agency such as NASA to launch effectively into this particular kind of language game. Nor does it require any advanced degree in futurology for predicting or creating a desired outcome for such dialogue. On the other hand, those of us in ministry, spiritual leadership, or chaplaincy in its various forms could have something to learn from the World Food Programme as it struggles to predict food shortages around the world, or NASA in its staging of complex programs for space exploration. In particular, they teach us something about the importance of goal setting and alert us to the fact that different goals require different methods for achieving them.

One of the things that has genuinely surprised me in studying theological reflection over the years are the many and sometimes radically diverse purposes it is intended to achieve, even in its "classical" Christian forms. For example, in one of the earlier books on the topic, Raymond Collins presents a series of models for theological reflection (see textbox 3.1). Embedded in the

TEXTBOX 3.1

Titles	Goals
The efficiency model	How do we make ministry more efficient?
The ecclesial model	What kind of Church do you want?
The Christological model	What Jesus does our ministry reflect?
The scriptural model	How does God's word critique our ministry?
The anthropological model	Is Christian ministry truly human?

Constructed from the work of Collins 1984.

title and question posed by each model are implicit and quite distinctive goals of each of these forms of theological reflection.

Choosing a model without giving due consideration to the purpose or purposes for which it is going to be employed could generate a whole variety of unintended and even unwelcome effects. For example, I have a personal penchant for things well organized and strive for an economy of time and energy when tackling a project: not surprisingly, my father was an industrial engineer and a time efficiency expert!

Let's imagine that I am leading a group of folk from my local congregation in a process of TR for the purpose of building greater harmony and respect between community members or, alternately, so we might discover how our congregation can more effectively contribute toward creating a safer environment for the children and teens in our neighborhood. As the facilitator of such processes, every bone in my body might be screaming, "Efficiency model! Efficiency model!" However, it is quite likely that such a model provides inadequate tools and even wrongheaded presuppositions for achieving our designated goals. The drive for efficiency, in all probability, could derail the whole undertaking.

Brooklyn-born psychologist Abraham Maslow wisely remarked that "I suppose it is tempting, if the only tool you have is a hammer, to treat everything as if it were a nail" (1966, 15). The key insight in this aphorism is that every instrument leaves its mark on a project, whether that project is designing a boat or disclosing belief. Similarly, every method one employs for a language game like reflective believing has an impact on the unfolding of that game. Thus, one must choose wisely what path to follow in unfolding one's own beliefs, or assisting others to do the same.

One of my conversions in this rethinking of the relationship between the widely differing purposes of TR and their complementary methods is a growing awareness that learning or even acquiring notable proficiency in a single method of TR—no matter how tested and proven that method—is probably no longer adequate. The shifting spiritual terrain and even hybridity of believing in the twenty-first century requires chaplains, ministers, and multiple other types of spiritual leaders to develop a certain methodological agility here. For example, as much as I appreciate the Whiteheads' model and method for TR, I also recognize that it is a process designed for achieving some pastoral action or spiritual resolution in the face of a particular need or crisis. It may not be well suited, however, for personal transformation or building friendships across some perceived religious divide, both of which can be valid goals for reimagined forms of TR.

This does not mean that chaplains or other types of reflective guides should not have a preferred method or two for their own personal reflection or for engaging others in the same. On the other hand, instinctively playing our methodological trump suit without assessing critically the purposes of the language game before us could raise the toll on this communicative highway higher than some of our intended dialogue partners are willing to pay. In the language of a former mentor, it is important "to see the light before choosing the path"; in other words, first discern the *why* of the process before deciding upon a *how*.

Throughout the remainder of this chapter, we will consider three distinctive scenarios for engaging in reflective believing: marriage preparation, interfaith hospital chaplaincy, and congregational leadership around an act of public theology. The marriage preparation was an experience in which I participated, and the congregational leadership incident was an experience of a former student who has given permission for the version presented here. Both of these retellings have been somewhat altered to mask the identities of those involved. The hospital chaplaincy incident is a fictionalized account that draws upon the real experiences of two former students and one clinical pastoral education (CPE) supervisor. The original information in this story has also been masked in this retelling. These case studies in service of reimagined forms of TR will allow us to explore something of the range of purposes that motivate acts of reflective believing. They will also reveal that quite often multiple purposes for such reflection can converge around the same event. This extended consideration of the purposes for RB and the way they often cluster together will then prepare us in the coming chapter to consider the cluster of head, hand, and heart skills important for developing competency as a reflective believer.

PREPARING TO SAY "I DO"

We will call them Fareed and Katherine, although those are not their real names. I met them through a referral from a staff member at the large urban parish where I frequently preach and lead worship. They had made an inquiry about being married at the church and wondered if there was a clergy person available for some counseling about the upcoming wedding. The staff member thought that maybe I could help them in marriage preparation. One of the first things I try to do when I meet with a couple in marriage preparation is to invite them into a storytelling mode of sharing about themselves. Here is part of the story that I heard.

Fareed is the youngest of three children, an only boy with two older sisters. His parents came to the United States from India before he was born and settled in southern California. He describes them as "relatively devout Muslims," but does not think of himself as being as devout or religious as they are. Fareed's father is a physician, and he is as well, just completing his residency at a prestigious hospital in the Midwest. His oldest sister is also a physician, and his other sister is an attorney.

Katherine is from a large Irish Catholic family from the south side of Chicago. The oldest of six children, she is currently finishing medical school in Chicago. Her father is a factory worker, and her mother is a teacher at the Catholic grade school that Katherine attended. She describes her entire family as "very Catholic" and recalls a home environment that was filled with family devotions and rituals. Katherine began to question her faith when she was in Catholic high school, and by the end of college thought of herself as a "recovering Catholic." She attends church when she visits her family on feasts like Christmas, but otherwise is disengaged from religion and mostly focused on getting into the right residency program.

They met when Katherine was on her first medical rotation at the hospital in which Fareed was a resident. Needless to say, they hit it off. After Katherine completed her rotation, she and Fareed began to date, and a year later they decided to marry. When I met with them for the first time, they explained that the wedding would not take place for at least another year or more, since Katherine needed to finish her last few months of medical school and get matched to a residency program. It was probable that she would be moving out of Chicago for her residency, and Fareed would have to decide if he would move as well.

Their immediate concern in our first meeting was the wedding ceremony itself, or more probably the two wedding ceremonies they might need to arrange. Fareed had attended a number of Christian and Catholic weddings, so he was somewhat familiar with the basic ritual and some of the traditions. For her part, Katherine had been reading up on the *Nikah* ceremony and had even watched different versions of that ceremony on YouTube. They wanted my opinion on the pros and cons of staging two different marriage ceremonies in two different parts of the country: a Catholic Mass in Chicago for Katherine's family and friends, and a *Nikah* in southern California for Fareed's family and friends.

I felt comfortable strategizing with them about the ritual. At the same time, it seemed that before they could choose an appropriate ritual path, they first needed to "see the light" and discern some of the purposes their rituals would need to address. Clearly, I was nudging them into a form of reflective believing in ritual mode. Furthermore, I suggested to them that, if they were to be effective, whatever rituals they crafted would have to address the needs of others besides themselves. Both Katherine and Fareed are close to their families and instinctively understood that it was not just the two of them marrying each other; in truth, families actually marry families.

We began this journey into reflective believing by having Fareed describe the *Nikah* ceremony as they were envisioning it. The ceremony would not take place at his parents' mosque but at some other venue where the non-Muslim guests—including Katherine's family—might feel more comfortable; they were also hoping that a different venue could also accommodate a reception that would follow the ceremony. While the *Nikah* traditionally takes place between the guardian of the bride and the groom, they would not employ such an intermediary. The ceremony would include the reading of the marriage contract, an exchange of consent between them, reciting verses from the Qur'an, an instruction, and a series of prayers and blessings. This would be followed by the reception for them and their guests.

Katherine then described her idea of a traditional Catholic marriage ceremony in the context of a Catholic Mass. She had images of her father walking her down the aisle and multiple ideas about who would be in the relatively large wedding party. I added that, as in the *Nikah*, there would be scriptural readings, and blessings, as well as communion. Unlike the *Nikah*, however, which has few prescribed elements, the Catholic Mass is quite well defined and legally prescribed. For example, in the Chicago Archdiocese it must take place in a Catholic church, and since Fareed and his family members were not baptized, they could not share in communion.

They were both a little shocked about the ritual and legal restrictions for a Roman Catholic wedding Mass, so I asked them to imagine what the two ceremonies might feel like, not only for them but also for their family and friends. How might Fareed's family feel in a Catholic church, not knowing the many responses or congregational prayers that punctuate the Catholic Mass, maybe unsure of what to do when Katherine's family knelt during parts of it, and not being allowed to take communion?

Inviting them to imagine these two ceremonies, and the feelings they might spark in each other and their families has some affinity with Killen and de Beer's approach to TR. The goal is not to make any immediate decision but to engage in some careful imagining while attending to the feelings such imaging might evoke as a way to think about possible directions for these ceremonies. I also noted that sometimes the *Nikah* is a religious ceremony that is not recognized by civil law, but the Catholic ceremony is recognized by the state. They were clearly unhappy that one ceremony carried that kind of civil recognition and not the other.

Killen and de Beer also believe that TR should invite people to make decisions that are grounded in important values, and reflect a level of integrity between the choices one makes and a life pattern grounded in those values (see textbox 3.2). In that vein, I asked them to think about what the two ceremonies might say publicly about present and future believing, and whether they felt a sense of coherence between what the rituals symbolically announced and how they were subsequently going to live out their lives. For example, both ceremonies employed sacred texts to frame their marriage: Would those

"How can I ground my decisions in the values that are important
to me? . . . Is there a way to find meaning in my life so that my
choices do not seem random but reflect an integral pattern? Is the
meaning in my life only my private possession or is it connected
to others?" (Killen and de Beer 1994, 1; see also appendix 1C)

scriptures play a role in their future lives? The Catholic ceremony asks, "Will
you accept children lovingly from God and bring them up according to the
law of Christ and his church?": do they agree with that basic presupposition?
If they feel drawn to begin their marriage with two religious ceremonies, to
what extent will religion or religious ritual play a role in their lives and that of
their children? Will Lent and Ramadan be observed? Easter and *Eid al-Fitr*?
If so—like the imagined two ceremonies—will such religious observances
be segregated to one side of the family or the other? How will this shape the
views of their children about the mutual interplay of these different religions?

Through this storytelling, imagining and reflecting upon feelings and patterns of belief, Fareed and Katherine thought that maybe a single ceremony,
weaving both traditions and both sides of the family together, might be a more
effective ritual option. It might also give them a model for envisioning how a
more integrative form of believing might emerge in their own home and family.
From my perspective, this encounter also illustrated that engaging in reflective
believing has multiple purposes, some of them more central than others. For
example, reflecting through the ritual seemed to reveal that there were important goals for the couple themselves. Primarily those appeared to be the need for
expressing and deepening their love of each other; a secondary goal might have
been discovering the integrity between their believing and the public ritualizing
of that belief. They also had a ritual "problem" to solve in terms of designing
appropriate worship for their wedding. As both were closely connected to their
families, it is clear they were also intent on building up good will, respect, and
common ground between them, and maybe even softening a few hearts. While
it was never explicitly mentioned, I also wondered whether the ritual design
that emerged was a symbol of liberation—especially for Katherine—from some
family expectations around religion and worship.

Reflective believing as a rhizomatic language game seldom follows a single trajectory and like life itself and that paradigmatic ginger root, takes many twists and turns. On the other hand, when respected and deployed as an improvisatory art, RB can display the nimbleness and agility to reverence the winding road of living and believing and even weave them together in an honorable coherence.

THE HOLY SPIRIT AS A BUDDHIST GIFT

Meredith is a twenty-seven-year-old Buddhist who has completed two years of divinity school. Born in Orlando, Florida, she grew up in a home without religion, although her grandmother was a devout evangelical Christian. She opines that her grandmother's strong piety was probably a little too much for her mother, who was raised and even married in an evangelical church, but never went back. Thus, her own home was devoid of religious practices and even talk about things religious. However, she did grow up with a strong sense of social justice. Like her mother, Meredith thought that teaching—especially in impoverished areas—was the best way for her to make a contribution to society. She completed a B.A. in early childhood education and then volunteered for Teach for America. She ended up teaching for four years in Oakland, California, and while she is deeply grateful for the experience, through it all she became somewhat disillusioned with teaching in a public school.

While in college, Meredith began exploring Eastern religions and developed a habit of meditating. While teaching in Oakland she became friends with a Japanese American Buddhist who invited her to a Sunday *Dharma* service with her family. Meredith felt immediately at home in this gathering, even though she was one of the only members who was not of Japanese descent; she soon became a regular member of this Buddhist community. Her involvement with this community got her thinking about becoming a Buddhist minister or chaplain. She considered pursuing a program in Buddhist studies, but was also very interested in interfaith work. Consequently, when she completed her second contract with Teach for America she applied and was accepted into a divinity school that celebrates the diversity of backgrounds and beliefs of its students and faculty. That is where she is now pursuing her ministerial goals.

After her second year in an M.Div. program, Meredith opted to complete a unit of clinical pastoral education during the summer through the spiritual care program at a large local hospital. She was the only Buddhist intern, but found the interfaith outlook of the staff and especially her supervisor—a pastor in the United Church of Christ—very welcoming. As part of her internship, Meredith regularly visited people on a floor devoted primarily to surgical patients. That is where she met Mrs. Hattie Johnson. According to the information available to her before the visit, Meredith knew that Mrs. Johnson was an African American in her late sixties who identified herself as a member of a local congregation in the Assembly of God tradition. She also knew that Mrs. Johnson was being prepared for some kind of surgery, but Meredith did not know more than that. This is part of the dialogue of her visit with Mrs. Johnson that she shared with her CPE colleagues and supervisor:

M: Hi, Mrs. Johnson, I am Meredith, a student chaplain at the hospital this summer. I just stopped by to say hello and see how you are doing, or if you needed anything.

J: Thank you, I could always use a little prayer; I'm going to have surgery tomorrow on my stomach, which is all blocked up, so I'm a little worried.

M: So you feel worried. That seems perfectly normal before surgery. Do you know if you will be unconscious or awake during the procedure?

J: Oh, honey, they are gonna knock me out. I just hope I wake up on the other side. I've never had surgery before.

M: I haven't either, and I can understand the worry. But our doctors here are very good, and I am sure they will take care of you, and I will come back to visit when you come out of surgery to see how you are doing.

J: That is very sweet.

M: So you asked for prayers. Have you been praying yourself?

J: Oh my, yes, I've been asking Jesus to send his healing on me. I've been praying for healing.

M: Good for you. I am from a different religious tradition, but love the concept of Jesus' spirit as a gift of healing.

J: What tradition are you, honey?

M: I'm a Buddhist, Mrs. Johnson.

GOAL SETTING FOR REFLECTIVE BELIEVING

J: Really? There are Buddhist chaplains?

M: Oh, there are all sorts of chaplains here and at other hospitals, just like there are people from all sorts of faiths here.

J: Well, that's true, and it does make sense. Everybody needs a little help from the Lord.

M: I don't know any prayers from your tradition, but I would be happy to spend a moment in quiet with you, hoping that in that quiet you might experience the calm and strength of the spirit of Jesus.

J: That would be very sweet.

M: Do you mind if I hold your hand in the quiet?

J: No, I'd like that.

[Meredith takes Mrs. Johnson's right hand in her two hands, and stands with her eyes closed in silence for a minute or so.]

M: I hope you experience the calm and the healing you are praying for, Mrs. Johnson.

J: That was good, just good. Thank you. I liked the quiet.

M: I will see you after the surgery, Mrs. Johnson. Be well.

J: Thank you, dear.

In reflecting upon the dialogue with the other interns and her supervisor, Meredith talked about wanting to respect Mrs. Johnson's own faith tradition while also trying to bring the resources of her own heritage to bear in the moment. She had done some reading about the Holy Spirit in an M.Div. course she took on the Protestant Reformation and John Calvin. More than that, however, she was drawing on the writings of one of her favorite authors, the Vietnamese Buddhist monk Thich Nhat Hanh. She remembered that Hanh, in his book *Living Buddha, Living Christ*, made a connection between the Buddhist practice of mindfulness and the healing spirit of Jesus (see textbox 3.3). While she did not feel that she could pray for Mrs. Johnson, she did feel that the gift of quiet and meditation from her tradition could provide a context in which Mrs. Johnson could pray for healing and experience some calming of her anxiety.

TEXTBOX 3.3

"To me, mindfulness is very much like the Holy Spirit. Both are agents of healing. When you have mindfulness, you have love and understanding, you see more deeply, and you can heal the wounds in your own mind. The Buddha was called the King of Healers. In the Bible, when someone touches Christ, he or she is healed. It is not just touching a cloth that brings about a miracle. When you touch deep understanding and love, you are healed." (Hanh 2007, 14–15)

Meredith's practice of reflective believing in this brief encounter with Mrs. Johnson revealed a constellation of purposes, some of which were quite different from those we observed with Fareed and Katherine. In some ways, this form of reflective believing could be understood as a gentle form of personal problem solving. The "problem" was Mrs. Johnson's anxiety in the face of impending surgery. Akin to some of the steps in the Whitehead model and method (see appendix 1D), Meredith was attentive to the feelings of Mrs. Johnson and her request for prayer. She also reached into the resources of Mrs. Johnson's religious heritage about the spirit of Jesus, as well as her own heritage of mindfulness and healing. By putting those two traditions in a practical dialogue, she was able to invite Mrs. Johnson's prayer, without violating the principles of her own tradition, which does not hold for a God who hears prayers. In the process, Meredith instinctively pursued a cluster of goals that we might identify as healing, accompaniment, connectedness to Mrs. Johnson's anxiety, hope building, and engaging the significance of the impending surgery in her life. One could similarly read this text as a way in which Meredith was trying to become a better practitioner of her own religious tradition in a quite integrated way.

For religious leaders, spiritual guides, and chaplains from various traditions, pastoral care encounters such as this are often opportunities for improvising powerful moments of reflective believing. When people are in crises, experiencing anxiety, or faced with important decisions, they are often more open to reflecting about deep values and befriending the resources of their spiritual heritage than at other times in their lives. As demonstrated in this partly fictionalized dialogue, reflective believing is more than a cognitive exercise. It is consequently an often complex endeavor, especially for a pastoral minister attempting to accompany a person they may never have met before at a time of crisis or high anxiety such as Mrs. Johnson. This challenge is magnified in the chaordic context of what Daniel Schipani and Leah Dawn Bueckert call "interfaith spiritual care" (2010).

More than an exercise of intercultural care, this journey into "interfaith spiritual care" requires the chaplain to deploy her gifts of interpathy not only across cultures and contexts but also across forms of believing that may or may not be consonant with the caregivers' own cultures or contexts. Having the capacity to befriend another's spiritual tradition with gratitude and respect while maintaining integrity around your own form of believing is an art that requires intelligence, skill, and authenticity. In the coming chapter we will further examine this constellation of capacities under the rubric of integration. Growing in this integrating art is enhanced by disciplined reflection and often by the guidance of a wise mentor who is both experienced in navigating this largely unexplored territory and capable of sharing the deep wisdom that comes from the joys and sorrows of such a journey.

BASKETBALL AND PUBLIC THEOLOGY

Young-Soo Kim was a youth pastor in the Presbyterian Church of Korea (PCK) before he joined our Ecumenical Doctor of Ministry program. When he entered the program, as with all other students, he was required to write a ministry incident report that related some previous ministerial experience in which he was a central figure and that continued to inspire or challenge him. With his permission, I will retell something of the story he told—masking all identities in the process. This story became a source of rich and eye-opening reflection for Kim as well as those of us who journeyed with him through the Ecumenical Doctor of Ministry program.

After graduating from the seminary, Kim was hired in the late 1990s by a Presbyterian church located in a small rural town, outside of a thriving urban center in South Korea. His primary responsibility was to minister to the fifteen- and sixteen-year-old students—or "fixteens"—in the parish. He had done this type of ministry before, on a part-time basis, while he was a senior seminarian in Seoul. He soon discovered, however, that these students would be quite unlike those he had previously experienced. Kim came to believe that this was true because the context and dynamics of this small town were very different from those of Seoul. Seoul is a bustling metropolis filled with modernistic skyscrapers, sprawling open markets, high-end shopping, and a myriad of museums, temples, and cultural opportunities. In this rich and admittedly highly competitive environment, Kim found his students motivated, engaged, and optimistic about their future. Such was not the case in his new home.

Kim described his new residence as a small town that operated as a kind of two-way bridge into the neighboring urban center. On the one hand, it was a place where people with unfulfilled hopes and dreams, having lived in the outlying areas for some time, planned their escape into the promise and potential of the city. On the other hand, it was also a place to which people, whose employment or financial dreams failed in that urban environment, often retreated in disappointment. Thus, a significant percentage of the residents are really not invested in this small town and are either on their way out of it or back living there only reluctantly. Furthermore, there is some tension between the small core population of residents, concerned about the stability of their community, and the more transient residents.

With his fixteens caught in this social limbo, Kim thought that his ministerial task was to bring his passion for God and the Christian gospel to them, so that they might develop a deep love of God and also a parallel love of neighbor. This path, however, did not prove to be terribly fruitful. Kim's senior pastor was very committed to his church's engagement in the local community and had some conversations with him about possible paths for meeting this need. Kim suggested that if they were going to engage the teens, it had to be around some issue or activity that they liked and one in which they could experience a sense of accomplishment and success. So when the senior pastor asked, "What interests them?" almost without thinking Kim said, "Sports!" The pastor thought this was insightful, and said, "Our kids do like soccer, baseball, and basketball. Yet soccer and baseball need many people to play and big fields. Basketball only needs five people, so maybe that is the direction in which we should go." Kim agreed, but thought that sometimes even trying to put together two teams of five players was challenging. Yet it was possible to play a half court basketball game with only three players on a team. Thus, it was decided: the new "ministry" would be three-on-three basketball.

The fixteens were very excited about this new project and threw their hearts and souls into three-on-three. They began drawing up lists of possible referees, making signs that could be posted in every middle and high school in the region, sending out official notifications to all the small towns in their area, and creating an application form on the congregation's website. Applications started pouring in. Kim also knew, however, that there was a serious problem that had to be faced.

While there are basketball courts in some of the schools and in some of the nearby cities, there were none in their town. Traveling to other places would make it difficult for the fixteens to manage the program and would also undercut a basic goal here: to help the teens develop an interest in their own town. Kim proposed, and the pastor agreed, that they would build a full-size basketball court and one half court on church property. That was an expensive venture, however, and had to be approved by the church's board of elders. That is where Kim ran into trouble.

Mr. Park was a long-standing elder in the church and a key person on the church's board. When Kim met with the church board for the first time to present his plan, it was Mr. Park who spoke up: "Pastor Kim, we know about your plan for basketball. It is announced all over the town and in our neighboring cities. Now you want us to approve money for building basketball courts, but you never even had the courtesy to tell us your plan before announcing it to the world." Kim later reflected that Korea is a nation where Confucian ideals are still very important, including honoring one's elders. Kim had never attended a meeting of the elders and thought that maybe the senior pastor who regularly met with them would have spoken of the plan. He had not, and consequently it appeared that Kim was the young assistant pastor who was undercutting the authority of the elders—something too many young people in Korea were perceived to be doing. Kim tried to explain the value and purpose of the project, but he did not get very far at that meeting.

The following Sunday Kim met with Mr. Park in a prayer room at the church and offered a profound apology to him for his apparent disrespect. He also recognized that many church members, like Mr. Park, felt their responsibility was to grow the church and not invest in the town. As part of his apology, Kim reflected on the teaching and ministry of Jesus that reached beyond his own neighborhood and people. He employed a favorite quote from the Gospel of John about God having a love affair with the world (3:16), and not just a love affair with the Jewish people or the Christian church. Mr. Park was impressed and persuaded. He soon became Kim's most important ally on the church board. As the coach of a local soccer team, he understood many things about organizing sporting events.

Since the church board thought the expenses for building the facilities were too high, Elder Park suggested that they construct the courts out of clay, which was much cheaper. He helped Kim and the students acquire the materials and found a heavy iron roller that he could hook to the back of his car for packing the clay and evening the surface of the clay courts. When it rained, he even showed them how to sponge up the water and return the court to a playable condition. Kim's one-time foe had actually become, in his words, a bit of a miracle worker.

As the courts were being finished, applications came to a close. Forty-seven teams had applied to play. Kim called it a blessing all around. A few days before the tournament began Kim held a worship event on the new courts. There, with his students and some of their parents and friends, they prayed in gratitude for the way their community had come together and in hope that the events would progress favorably. In the final days they drew the lines on the courts, created a first aid station and concession stand, and developed all the protocols for checking players' identification, keeping time, and recording the scores and results for the head office. On a glorious Saturday afternoon, the first games began at 2:00 p.m. and continued over three weekends.

This successful beginning of the church's explicitly non-religious involvement with the local town has continued. In addition to three-on-three basketball, the church has subsequently staged many different kinds of sporting events for the sake of building a sense of community in this small town, including badminton, ping-pong, and *Jokgu*—a very popular South Korean sport that is a fusion of volleyball, soccer, and tennis.

Pastor Young-Soo Kim later remarked that the Presbyterian Church of Korea has often become focused on its own growth and the salvation of individual members of its congregation. However, he believes that the church has a responsibility to help all peoples live together in harmony—another important Confucian value. He believes that the three-on-three basketball initiative not only contributed to such an aim but also shaped a group of young people to understand that they had a responsibility, even a mission, to serve the wider community, whether members of that wider community shared their religious values and faith tradition or not.

Compared with the stories about Fareed and Katherine, and Meredith and Mrs. Johnson, this example of reflective believing has a much broader scope. Instead of a form of pastoral care or family ministry, it might best be understood as a form of "public theology" (see textbox 3.4). The term *public theology* was introduced by Lutheran theologian Martin Marty. It is related to his image of the "public church." As he defined it, this decidedly Christian image was a church not so much concerned with saving individuals or reconciling them to God but with helping to constitute civil, social, and political life employing the resources of faith (Marty 1981, 16).

Some forms of reflective believing are clearly at the service of individual needs or designed to enable families or small communities to cope with internal challenges and anxieties. Other forms of reflective believing, however, are more centrifugal, with a focus on the wider community or social context in which many kinds of believers have both an interest and a stake. Privileging this wider context as an arena for bringing one's values to bear—whether those are the values of a humanist, a member of the Baha'i faith or an Episcopalian—implicates a different set of goals and suggests different methods for achieving such goals. Kim's project was clearly focused on community building, engaging what some call the "dialogue of life," and promoting the common good. It was employing a form of recreation (three-on-three basketball) as a means for re-creating a community. It also seemed intent on building hope in that small town. Finally, there seemed to be a mutually enriching process in which one particular church broadened its perspective on ministry and, in turn, enabled one local community to broaden its perspective on the potential gifts and contributions of a local church to the common good.

Employing an approach that some liberation theologians such as Joe Holland and Peter Henriot call "the pastoral circle" (see appendix 1B), achieving such goals first requires an immersion or insertion into a context where one experiences the social issues at hand. Kim's move from Seoul to his rural community was akin to such an immersion experience. Immersion leads to social analysis, or Kim's growing awareness of his small town as a "two-way

TEXTBOX 3.4

Public theology "refers to the engagement of a living religious tradition with its public environment—the economic, political and cultural spheres of our common life." (Benne 1995, 4)

bridge" that discouraged people from investing in their community. This engendered a kind of theological reflection that led to an unusual form of pastoral action. Admittedly, Kim was not consciously following Holland and Henriot's method, just as Meredith was not trying to evoke the model and method of the Whiteheads, nor was I even conscious of borrowing insights from Killen and de Beer during discussions with Fareed and Katherine. Much of the methodological turn, especially as one develops competence as a reflective believer, is instinctive and improvisatory, a topic to which we will turn in our last chapter. The practices of effective leaders are nonetheless revelatory of some juggling of knowledge and skills available to those of us who wish to engage in such service, and underscore that the path or *how* of proceeding is ordinarily enlightened by the *why* of proceeding.

COMPOUND EYES AND SACRED HEARTS

The world of animals and insects is a source of endless fascination for me. There are frogs that can spontaneously change their gender, transparent creatures that inhabit the deepest trenches of the ocean, and some birds that can dive over 150 feet into water while others can actually fly over the Himalayas. One anatomical feature of insects that is enviable and enlightening is the compound eye that most of them have. According to the Hooper Virtual Paleontological Museum (2013), these eyes are composed of hundreds or even thousands of facets, each facing in a slightly different direction. Each facet records a general impression of the color and intensity of the light but does not produce a complete image. Every facet is connected directly to the insect's brain and contributes one spot of light to the image, much as tiles do in a mosaic. There are several advantages to such an eye. One is its ability to produce a multiscopic rather than stereoscopic view of the landscape. Another is its efficiency in processing images and assimilating changes very quickly. To such an insect, a Hollywood movie would look like a series of still photographs, and a magician's hand trick would be completely transparent to the compound eye.

Analogously, those wishing to engage or lead reflective believing in this chaordic context would be well served by developing a kind of compound inner eye, or better yet, a compound heart. A compound heart is one that has the capacity for interpathic beating across cultures, contexts, and forms of believing that might at first seem odd, and maybe even completely unreasonable, to us. A compound heart in the face of such diversity beats more effectively if it is resonant with what some faith traditions call "a sacred heart." Such a metaphorical heart is capable of remaining open through reimagined forms of theological reflection that serve many, diverse, and even what might appear to be opposite purposes. Reflective believing worthy of the name is not an exclusivist exercise designed for achieving only a narrowly defined set of goals. As discussed in chapter 1, limiting RB in such a way seems like a move toward what Deleuze and Guattari might characterize as "arboreal" rather than as "rhizomatic," the latter of which seems more attuned to the pluriform modes of believing in the current age.

In a variety of consultations on this topic with theological educators, M.Div. students, field supervisors, and others, I have often employed an exercise that entailed handing out a page that listed some of the many possible purposes of RB. Textbox 3.5 is one of the fruits of that exercise. On the page that I shared with consultants there was a place for them to note whether they agreed, disagreed, or were not sure about each of the various goals. In one consultation, none of the participants affirmed "friendship" as a possible goal of any reimagined form of theological reflection, and several objected to it as an inappropriate goal. Weeks later I met with Cassie Meyer at the Interfaith Youth Core in Chicago. She told me that one of the things that spurred her into interfaith work was an experience in college. She identified herself as a conservative evangelical but found herself at a college with a student population representing a wide range of belief systems. She relates that she became friends with a Muslim from Bangladesh, and thought that she should invite him to think about Jesus. Surprisingly, during one of their conversations, before she could broach the topic, he tried to convert her to Islam. This turned out to be a very funny experience for both of them, as her colleague Eboo Patel relates in *Sacred Ground* (2012, 134–35). What was most touching for me in her personally relating of that story before I read it was that the motivation for her engaging in interfaith dialogue, for entering in the journey that I call reflective believing (2012), was her interest in sustaining and fostering friendship with this obviously pious and very good-hearted Muslim.

A journey into reflective believing is a form of spiritual eye surgery, transplanting the stereoscopic eye with a compound one. It is a metaphorical willingness to open-heart surgery that adjusts a heart that beats to one vision of religion or forms of believing to beat interpathically across a dazzling and enriching terrain defined by and around religion. Its motto or maybe mantra could be "No trees, just rhizomes, no trees, just rhizomes, no trees, just rhizomes."

TEXTBOX 3.5

POSSIBLE GOALS OF
REFLECTIVE BELIEVING

1. Integration
2. Transformation
3. Love of self
4. Healing
5. Discipleship
6. Love of other
7. Self-grounding
8. Becoming more human
9. Loving God
10. Recreation/re-creation
11. Problem solving
12. Community building
13. Apologetics
14. Liberation
15. Softening of hearts
16. Changing theology
17. Character building
18. Friendship
19. Giving a religious account of one's life
20. Self-knowledge
21. Accompaniment
22. Solidarity/connectedness
23. Broadening perspectives
24. Building hope
25. Raising up voices of marginalized
26. Conversion of life
27. Dialogue of life [nontheistic integration]
28. Strengthening faith
29. Connecting people with the cosmos
30. Eliminating religious privilege
31. Promoting the common good
32. Building respect
33. Becoming a better practitioner of my faith tradition
34. Engaging significance in people's lives
35. Making sense of suffering
36. Clarifying practice for the next challenge

Compiled by the author from multiple conversations and consultations, 2012–2013.

Believing with Head, Hands, and Heart

We do not act rightly because we have virtue or excellence, but we rather have these because we have acted rightly.

—*Will Durant (1926, 76)*

George Lucas opened his epic *Star Wars* series in 1977 with the memorable phrase, "A long time ago in a galaxy far, far away . . ." That is just about how I remember the beginning of my collegiate career when I was studying organ performance at a small Lutheran college in the Midwest: a long time ago in what seems galaxies away from my current life. I had begun organ studies in late adolescence, only at the end of high school. Although I had some dexterity at the keyboard, looking back it is clear that my playing was pretty erratic and certainly pedestrian. That assessment, however, was not in my consciousness as I approached my first "organ jury." Each semester all performance students at the school were required to play before the faculty members of their respective instrumental departments in order to prepare them for performing in the final recital required for graduation. Such juries were also intended to help acclimatize students to public music making, a necessary skill given that so many of us were preparing to be church musicians.

The chair of the organ department was a virtuoso at the keyboard—a student of world-renowned instructors, and subsequently recognized as a celebrated teacher himself. He was also a genuinely kind human being. When

I look back, it seems a grace that he was present at that formative stage of my life. In the jury I blasted through the little piece of Bach that I had prepared, thought the performance was quite good (after all, I had not hit an unusual number of wrong notes), and expected modest praise and encouragement from the faculty when it was over. It was silence, however, that greeted the end of that performance. After what seemed like an unusually long interval, the chair stood and respectfully inquired, "Mr. Foley, have you studied any music theory yet?" I replied that my music theory courses were to begin the next semester. He smiled and said, "Good, you'll play better after you've had some theory," and, to a chorus of nodding heads from the other faculty members, he sat down and sent me on my way.

In the decades following that memorable interchange, I have come to appreciate the many gifts embedded in such cryptic wisdom. A key revelation has been that engaging in performance—whether that be playing an instrument, ministering to a congregation or mentoring others in their quest for meaning—requires a combination of disparate and sometimes even competing skills and capacities. We have already hinted at some of those in the previous chapters—for example, in our consideration of abilities such as listening attentively and keeping silent; encountering the other with respect, even awe; and exercising an imagination that can propel empathy across cultures and context so that it is transformed into what David Augsburger called interpathy.

This chapter will provide a more comprehensive examination of how our thinking, feeling, and embodiment contribute to reflective believing that is both generative and generous. The aim here has some resonance with what we attempted in the previous chapter. There we suggested that amid the myriad purposes that could fuel this reflection, certain goals seemed to cluster together depending upon the hoped-for outcomes of such reflection. In an analogous way, we will here consider how various skills and types of capacities naturally converge in the process of reflective believing. More important than their convergence for simply *doing* RB, however, is their convergence on the journey to actually *becoming* a more adept and reflective believer. A common way of speaking about this convergence of skills and capacities in the doing and becoming in theological education is through the rubric of integration. In a spirit of full disclosure, it is one of the key goals of reflective believing for me as a theological educator. RB contributes to integration. At the same time, however, it strikes me that the practice of RB itself needs to be a process that both respects and integrates the various facets of our being and believing.

INTEGRATION

Almost as disputed as the term *theological reflection* is the language of integration (see textbox 4.1), which is widely employed by educators—particularly in theological education—but it is seldom defined with any care. Too often it is treated as a one-way expectation professors, supervisors, or formation directors have for the students in their care. When broadly conceived as a "student" task, it is often envisioned as a largely cognitive journey that seminarians or others in training for spiritual leaders undertake as they attempt to find connections across the theological curriculum, careening from topic to topic and seminar to seminar. A common example of a ministerial student making such cognitive connections is one who is encouraged to link what she learns in biblical exegesis with her preaching courses, or "integrate" what she is learning in ethics with the material currently covered in her course on community leadership.

Maybe it was my musical training in college and graduate school that provided the intuition for a more holistic understanding of integration. While always a mediocre musician, I was still surrounded by gifted peers and professors who, for example, knew the history of Mozart and the musical scene in which he flourished, could analyze the form and harmonic language of his piano concerti, and were articulate about performance theory. More astonishing, however, was the fact that they could beautifully execute his Piano Concerto no. 23 in A Major with the university orchestra. One particular professor who had all of these classical skills was also a dazzling jazz musician. To hear him move from Beethoven to Brubeck, displaying both technical and improvisatory skills across that musical landscape, was awe-inspiring. This

---

TEXTBOX 4.1

"In general, integration refers to the bringing together of distinct entities or parts and in the process the creation of something new, a wholeness that exceeds the sum of its parts." (Cahalan 2012, 388)

interplay of mental acuity and manual dexterity, book knowledge, and body knowledge combined with affective expression and discipline—so far beyond my own musicianship—has remained for me an image of a more holistic form of integration. While not a performance artist in the traditional sense, I increasingly consider my teaching of presiding and preaching in public worship over the past three decades—as well as my own ministry as preacher and leader of worship—as a performing art. Teaching and leading various forms of reimagined theological reflection are, in my estimation, similar.

Performing arts such as ministry or reflective believing as well as the processes for becoming such a performing artist appear to be more effective when a series of skills and competencies are harmoniously brought to bear on the event. Since RB is a dynamic occurrence, which, as noted in chapter 2, might best be served through the language of verbs and gerunds, here we similarly suggest that the noun *integration* is less appropriate language than that of *integrating*.

My recovering alcoholic friend, whose quip about "having to be somewhere before Christmas" I cited in that same chapter, is insistent that the work of "recovery" is not achieved until death. He notes that for an alcoholic to proclaim that he "is recovered" or "has achieved recovery" is to doom himself to relapse. Alcoholics Anonymous has taught him that he will be "recovering" for the rest of his mortal existence. Similarly, for Buddha and Jesus and Mohammed, the journey of spiritual integrating that each of them undertook was the task of a lifetime, and maybe even more.

Juggling

Because integration is often treated as a largely cognitive or other narrowly circumscribed capacity, over the years I have migrated toward a more tangible and even playful metaphor for capturing something of the process of integrating: that of juggling. While I personally have never been able to keep three objects simultaneously whirling in midair for more than a few seconds, the ability to juggle has always captivated me. It is fascinating to watch some juggler take three or four or more small colored balls and maintain them in gravity-defying motion overhead without giving even the hint of exertion. Even more exciting, of course, is the growing anticipation that this is just the beginning of the routine and more challenging moves are yet to come. Maybe the acrobat will substitute a few rings or wine bottles or bowling pins

for those small colored balls, and as the act progresses you're hoping for flam-
ing torches or some other hazardous objects rotating above for the big finish.
Besides the manual dexterity of the art, I am equally fascinated by what might
be considered the sociology of juggling. Parallel to our journey into believing,
some people juggle alone while others juggle in pairs or in groups, standing
next to each other or even on each other's shoulders.

Juggling is not simply a metaphor for the process of ministerial integration
for me, but also a rich image for negotiating a balanced and interdependent
life while maintaining some semblance of inner calm and peacefulness. I have
a relative, for example, who astounds me with her ability to manage work
and children, friends and family, household and church in realistic, yet life-
giving, ways. Observing her clarifies for me that juggling is not the same thing
as multitasking. Multitasking can be reduced to the simultaneous execution
of several tasks while too often devoting little thought or reflection to them,
even though they could benefit from that attention: as when a student is taking class notes while simultaneously answering e-mail. Juggling life as a form
of integrating requires much more consideration and even a kind of practical
wisdom that is quite different from the mechanical or organizational dexterity that makes multitasking possible.

For example, my relative has a very smart and somewhat demanding four-
year-old granddaughter, Maddie. Observing her negotiate with Maddie in a
way that moves her toward a decision that is mutually acceptable to both of
them without dominating or demeaning the child is eye opening, especially
for someone who has never had children. It exemplifies to me a honed capacity for what Bonnie Miller-McLemore calls "sloppy mutuality" (2004),
or that distinctive form of mutual regard that people of unequal power or
capacities—such as parents and teachers—need to exercise. Observing her
exercise such mutual regard with so little apparent effort while keeping the
home office afloat and her staff productive and affirmed while starting dinner
preparations on the side makes me wonder why she is not the one training
students in the ministerial arts rather than me.

While there are multiple frameworks for thinking about RB as a form
of juggling in the service of integrating, the triangulation of head, hand,
and heart will provide a basic map for this consideration. Sometimes these
three interweaving forms of intelligence are named as *orthodoxy* or "right
believing," *orthopraxy* or "right acting," and *orthopathy* or "right feeling." So

named, they can seem like three separate human operations that are accomplished sequentially (i.e., if I develop the right beliefs they will lead me to the right practices that will leave me with the right feelings).

Instead of treating these as though they are distinctive human operations that cumulatively lead to some desirable result or feeling, however, I envision them much more intertwined and interactive, akin to the teaching from my own religion's tradition about the mystery of God that many Christians call the Trinity. Traditional Christian teaching, expressed in ancient creeds, holds that the Trinity is composed of three distinctive "persons" who are "one in being." Over the centuries this impenetrable mystery has been represented by everything from St. Patrick's shamrock to fiction writer William P. Young's imaginative triad of an African American woman, a Middle Eastern carpenter, and an Asian woman in his bestselling novel *The Shack* (2007). Maybe more dynamic than these natural symbols or personifications is an ancient insight from the Christian East that envisions the mystery in terms of dancing, or what in Greek is called *perichoresis*. This is the three-in-one in a dynamic interpenetration one of the other, which allows them to be distinctive without being separate, rendering each substantial as well as generous.

As recovered and reimagined by contemporary writers such as C. Baxter Kruger (2005), *perichoresis* is a dance of empathy and mutual regard that eliminates hierarchy or domination in the Godhead. In that respect, it has some clear resonance with the way Deleuze and Guattari employed the metaphor of a rhizome to reimagine a nonhierarchical form of conversation. As a kind of "sacred chaord," the Trinitarian *perichoresis* suggests a holy ordering without attempting to delimit or contain the divine spark that some of us call God. The generosity of this dance is manifest in the teaching that this energy is imagined as centrifugal rather than centripetal. It is decidedly not the closed activity of some transcendent Godhead accessible only to Christians, but an act of immanence as humanity itself is invited into the dance. I offer this image from my own tradition not because I expect every reader to agree with the teaching or even to understand it. Quite frankly, Christians do not completely understand it, which is why we call it a mystery. However, I find it an unusually rich analogy for personal and interpersonal juggling and integrating in the face of transcendence. Both the mobility and lack of hierarchy in the image are particularly attractive for me when thinking about the interplay of thinking, acting, and feeling. It is also one way for me to model—as with my earlier discussion of Jesus in chapter 1—how I endeavor to engage my own religious tradition in the reflective arts.

From my perspective it is somewhat problematic to treat orthodoxy, orthopraxis, and orthopathy separately. On one hand, each is an important facet for making the journey into reflective believing, which itself should be an integrating process. On the other hand, these are distinctive ways of being and knowing and it is beneficial to examine them individually. While attempting to define their distinctiveness in the coming pages, however, we will also emphasize their mutuality and interpenetration hopefully without creating any hierarchy or domination between them.

In order to underscore this intent, I will deviate from what some might consider the "logical" starting point and begin with orthopathy, not orthodoxy. I do this because too often in the Euro-American academic traditions—traditions that shaped me through decades of formal education—there is a distinctive prejudice for theoretical knowledge and cognitive skills that can tend to subordinate the doing and the feeling. The most glaring example of that in my own training is the fact that during all of the years of graduate work that prepared me to receive a doctoral degree in the area of worship, I was never once required to shape, lead, or even attend worship!

Prioritizing theory over practice, or cognition over affect often creates a form of "applied" reasoning. This type of thinking begins with harvesting ideas that have been incubating in the head—often in the head of the expert or teacher—and then attempting to put them into practice, often in the hands of novices or students. This theory > practice approach is quite typical in the training of ministers or other spiritual leaders who first study the history or systematic structure of beliefs or different religions and then are launched out into some supervisory situation in which they are expected to apply what they have learned in the classroom now out in a ministry or field of service. The language game of reflective believing and the integrating journey that enable us to be increasingly effective reflective believers, however, operates with a different set of rules. As we will explore, there are many ways of knowing. The quote from American philosopher Will Durant (d. 1981) at the beginning of this chapter—often misattributed to Aristotle (d. 322 BCE)—hints at this truth. Each way of knowing is valuable in its own right, and together they weave a richness of being and perception that is not possible when preempted by a single mode of reasoning. One of the ways of knowing that seldom finds a place in classical theologies or studies of believing is the affective way. Thus it is with orthopathy that we will begin.

ORTHOPATHY: HEARTS BEATING IN TUNE WITH THE COSMOS

One of the rituals required or those of us who grew up Roman Catholic was what we now call the Sacrament of Reconciliation. When I was a kid we called it "going to confession." Part of the preparation for confession was making an examination of conscience. Often these preparatory exercises were based on the ten commandments, or a list of the so-called seven deadly sins. Virtually all of those exercises—like many contemporary versions in print and on the Internet—offered questions about whether you had been angry or impatient, prideful or envious. As a consequence, I grew up believing that certain feelings were a sin and many times as a grade school student confessed, "I got angry at my older brother five times and was impatient with my little sister three times." You can imagine how shocked I was, years later, when I studied the Christian scriptures in depth and ran across the story of Jesus losing his temper and knocking over the tables of money changers in the temple (see textbox 4.2). How could Jesus be angry, I wondered; wasn't he supposed to be without sin?

Many theologies and even spiritualities consider feelings as potential obstacles to holiness. Thus, it is not surprising that few spiritual leaders or moral guides have a positive much less developed appreciation of human affections. One notable exception was the English cleric and theologian John

---

TEXTBOX 4.2

"The Passover of the Jews was near, and Jesus went up to Jerusalem. In the temple he found people selling cattle, sheep, and doves, and the money changers seated at their tables. Making a whip of cords, he drove all of them out of the temple, both the sheep and the cattle. He also poured out the coins of the money changers and overturned their tables. He told those who were selling the doves, 'Take these things out of here! Stop making my Father's house a marketplace!'" (John 2:13–16, *New Revised Standard Version of the Bible*)

Wesley (d. 1791). Wesley often spoke of religious or "holy" affections and considered his movement—eventually known as Methodism—as a religion of the heart. He once wrote that the religion that he longed to see established in the world was "a religion of love and joy and peace, having its seat in the heart, in the inmost soul" (Wesley 1987, 46). As many commentators have noted, Wesley was not seeking a spiritual reform based on the fleeting feelings that erupt and subside in us throughout the day without much thought or discipline. Rather, he recognized that there are deep logics in the body—different from those of the brain—that both foster and reveal the highest aspirations of humanity. Thus, even when our thinking is not clear and we are unable to reason our way into a proper practice or path, the human heart is a source of profound wisdom for showing the way.

Whether at the service of some theistic belief, or rooted in our deepest humanist instincts, what Gregory Clapper calls a "right heart" or *orthokardia* (1990) is both a boon to human development and foundational for reflective believing. In his previously cited work subtitled *A Non-Believer's Guide to the Uses of Religion*, Alain de Botton (2012) seems to recognize this as he devotes entire chapters to themes such as "kindness" and "tenderness." Furthermore, promoting such affections appears so important to de Botton that he believes that it should even permeate our modern architecture. Thus, for example, he argues that contemporary museums should rearrange their art collections so that, instead of displaying works according to genre or epoch, masterpieces are grouped so that they promote discerning affections such as love and compassion (de Botton 2012, 245).

One of the more unexpected arguments for such orthokardia comes from leadership gurus Ronald Heifetz and Marty Linsky, both on the faculty of the Kennedy School of Government at Harvard. They conclude their decidedly secular bestseller, *Leadership on the Line*—designed for CEOs, managers, politicians, and the like—with a final chapter resonant with an image we previously employed in chapter 3. It is surprisingly titled "Sacred Heart." They write:

> A sacred heart is an antidote to one of the most common and destructive "solutions" to the challenges of modern life: numbing oneself. Leading with an open heart helps you stay alive in your soul. It enables you to feel faithful to whatever is true, including doubt, without fleeing, acting out or reaching for a quick fix. Moreover, the power of a sacred heart helps you to mobilize others to

do the same—to face challenges that demand courage, and to endure the pains of change without deceiving themselves or running away. (Heifetz and Linsky 2002, 230)

While Killen and de Beer wisely understood that feelings have a distinctive role in their process of theological reflection (see appendix 1C), it is remarkable to me that humanist philosophies and secular leadership strategies recognize the significance of nurturing a "right heart" as well. The implication seems to be that if you are willing to wager on nurturing a heart tuned to the experiences and needs of others, then a new and unusual path of wisdom opens before you.

In some ways the litmus test for determining if one is nourishing such a sacred heart can be found in the virtues that both feed and flow from such a heart. Virtue language underscores our concern that we are not simply pondering some cursory emotions that erupt from our viscera whenever someone alternatively gives us a compliment or infuriates us with an insult. Aristotle is one who thought a great deal about virtues. He distinguished between virtues related to the mind and the moral virtues or virtues of character that are more closely related to what we are calling "heart." These moral virtues are not reducible to feelings but instead are dynamic capacities for making a proportionate response to the real events of life in view of our feelings. In *Nicomachean Ethics*, he explains this type of moral juggling by noting that a virtuous act is about acquiring some middle way, which is difficult. It requires figuring out how to act "at the right time, about the right things, towards the right people, for the right end, and in the right way" (Aristotle 2000, 2.6, 1106b, 18–22). He concludes that such activity is not easy and it is certainly not for everyone.

A critical virtue in this endeavor that we have already mentioned is that of humility. Teachers from Confucius (d. 479 BCE) to St. Augustine (d. 450 CE) have recognized the importance of this virtue and even consider it foundational for all others. While understood as a key to holiness or enlightenment by ancient and modern sages, we might be surprised to learn that contemporary research demonstrates that humility is also a pivotal factor in leadership. Management researcher Jim Collins, for example, believes he can empirically demonstrate that personal humility combined with professional will are essential ingredients for what he calls "level 5 leaders" (2005). That level of leadership, he explains, is one that is capable of taking a good company and making it great. Although it might seem counterintuitive, Collins argues that it is not personal ego and raw ambition that creates such leadership, but the ying and yang of humility and will.

For those engaged in the style of language game we characterized as theological inquiry in chapter 1, humility is an essential gift for pondering the transcendent. Many forms of believing, such as that of my own tradition, posit the necessary existence of many mysteries that will never be unraveled in this world, such as the Trinity that we discussed above. While we try to probe those mysteries, we do so with an intellectual modesty that from the beginning admits the inadequacy of our efforts. Cartoonist and cultural-religious pundit Charles Schulz crafted a number of comic strips pointedly featuring Snoopy as a theologian who deftly unmasked this essential attitude. One such cartoon depicts Snoopy on top of his doghouse writing a book on theology. Charlie Brown, when hearing of this new project, hopes aloud that Snoopy has a good title for this work. The enigmatic Snoopy concludes he has the perfect title: "Has it ever occurred to you that you might be wrong?" (Short 1990, 12). Those of us who write theological books are both devastated and invigorated by the prospects of that wondrous title.

The genre of humility needed for the language game we are calling reflective believing, however, is not simply an awareness of the inadequacy of our own thinking, or even that of the mystics or philosophers on whom we rely. Rather, it is more akin to what Swedish theologian and one-time dean of the Harvard Divinity School Krister Stendahl (d. 2008) called "holy envy." In 1985, there was significant opposition to the building of a temple by the Church of Jesus Christ of Latter-day Saints in Stockholm. As a retired bishop of Stockholm for the Church of Sweden, Stendahl responded to these protests at a 1985 press conference with what have come to be known as "Stendahl's three rules of religious understanding." Noting that the rules for good leadership are similar to these rules for interfaith dialogue, he later reiterated them as "(1) let the other define herself (don't think you know the other without listening), (2) compare equal to equal (not my positive qualities to the negative ones of the other), and (3) find beauty in the other so as to develop 'holy envy'" (Landau 2007, 30).

Holy envy is humility in an appreciative mode. It also opens a pathway for the other holy affections that well serve reflective believing. Some of these that we have previous mentioned include openness, respect, and empathy on its way to interpathy. This journey also requires much patience, both with ourselves and with our dialogue partners, be they our home community or some newly encountered pilgrim whose path might intersect with our own. It also seems difficult to embark upon this journey without a deep sense of hope, and a determined expectation that this clearly demanding venture might lead us to a more tolerant, even harmonious society. For theists, a hoped-for goal of this journey is also divine union, although we cannot expect or impose this goal upon all our honored dialogue partners.

This journey into holy affections and the virtues that mark them is not some necessary move into the politically correct, nor a calculated detour into the laughable and eventually dismissible realm of the "touchy-feely." Instead, this is an intentional right turn into ethics. This is a fundamental turn toward justice rooted in the human heart and nurtured through a moral sensitivity deeply planted in orthopathy. My colleague, John Pawlikowski, is an ethicist and for many decades the leader of the Jewish-Christian dialogue at my home institution. Reflecting on ethics in light of the *Shoah* or Jewish Holocaust of the mid-twentieth century, Pawlikowski offers powerful words about the centrality of right feeling for right thinking and acting. He writes,

> One of the convictions that has continued to deepen with me . . . is that moral sensitivity remains an indispensable prelude to moral reasoning. We ethicists can provide the necessary clarifications of human response mandated by such sensitivity. Such clarifications are absolutely essential if religious experience is not to degenerate into religious fanaticism. But, as an ethicist, I cannot create the sensitivity itself. Mere appeals to reason, authority, and/or natural law will prove ineffective by themselves. Such sensitivity will reemerge only through a new awareness of God's intimate link with human kind, in suffering and joy, through symbolic experience. Nothing short of this will suffice in light of the Holocaust. (Pawlikowski 2003, 169–70)

The invitation into orthopathy and the shaping of a right heart is clearly not the same as the developmental task of learning to discipline our emotions. While that is an important undertaking, the work of orthokardia demands more (i.e., the nurturing and sustaining of an authentic moral sensitivity). This moral sensitivity, grounded in humility, tunes us to the dignity of all people and the potential for good that resides in every heart. Authentic reflective believing presumes an ability to lead with such a heart.

ORTHOPRAXIS: BODIES IN MOTION

The Olympics have always fascinated me. More than professional or even collegiate sporting events, there is something about watching this spectacle of global athleticism that I find mesmerizing. One aspect that always confounds me is the incredible age range of Olympians at these events. In 2012, a seventy-one-year-old competed in dressage for Japan, and he was not the oldest in the history of the games. On the other hand, it is not a great surprise that the vast majority of medal winners at the last Olympics were in their early twenties. I had often heard that the human body naturally "peaks" for young adults around that age.

What I find astonishing, however, are the consistent number of teenagers who not only compete in the Olympics but also win medals. In 2012, for example, a fifteen-year-old named Alejandra Orozco Loza won a silver medal in diving. How does someone that young accomplish such a feat? One of the more famous child prodigies in international competitions was the Romanian gymnast Nadia Comăneci, who, at age thirteen, won four gold and one silver medal at the 1975 European championships. The following year, at the ripe old age of fourteen, she not only won three gold medals at the 1976 Montreal Olympics (including the all-around) but also scored a perfect 10.00 in the uneven bars—an Olympic achievement never before accomplished in modern gymnastics.

This excursus into Olympic history is not intended as some sporty diversion from the important topic at hand, but rather as a pointed illustration of the critical contribution of embodiment to integration. Very often academics—including many who teach in seminaries, divinity schools, and analogous professional training venues—give priority to head knowledge over praxis, suggesting that the acquisition of theory is necessary before one can adequately develop body skills. Olympic history, as well as the innumerable studies of top-level collegiate and even professional athletes, on the other hand, pointedly challenges such sequencing. Turning back to Nadia Comăneci, for example, one can seriously ask how much theoretical knowledge an almost fourteen-year-old could have acquired about kinesiology, sports psychology, or aerodynamics on her way to so many celebrated championships and medals. My guess is precious little. I am not suggesting that Comăneci was dumb by any means; on the contrary, her long and flourishing career as an athlete and businesswoman proves otherwise. Yet, while the darling of Montreal may not have possessed much theoretical knowledge about these elite fields of study, she did have what we could classify as an encyclopedic "body knowledge" about them.

There was also someone who for decades had displayed a gift for all of that head knowledge: that was Comăneci's famed coach, Béla Károlyi. Károlyi started training Nadia when she was seven years old and, except for a brief hiatus in the late 1970s, when she was coached by others with disastrous results, Károlyi mentored her throughout her astoundingly successful gymnastics career. Károlyi was a brilliant coach; yet he himself could not fly through routines like his protégé.

Similarly, Phil Jackson was a good professional basketball player, and even possesses two championship rings as a player to prove it. However, Jackson regularly admits that he could never hold a candle to his star players such as Michael Jordan or Kobe Bryant, who helped him achieve over five times as many championship rings as any other NBA coach (eleven in all). Then there is Bob Bowman, who never won an international swimming championship in his life but somehow coached Michael Phelps into winning a record-breaking twenty-two Olympic medals.

This synergy between coaches and athletes—akin to that between sages and disciples—demonstrates that head knowledge is important and cannot be dismissed. Yet it does not always have to reside in the performing body, which can achieve its own kind of knowing. Such synergy also suggests that the integrating process is not simply an individual journey, but a dynamic capacity that belongs to and is proctored by families, groups, and communities.

It is difficult for a novice to be on an effective integrating journey if her mentor is personally disintegrating. Similarly, the individual seminarian or ministry student needs the support of an institution committed to an integrating vision if the individual is to make progress along that path. As often as not, the litmus test for progress on this journey is not simply how one thinks, what is written in some thesis or appears as an institutional mission statement, but more often how individuals and communities perform. This certainly challenges the way that many educational ventures in the West prize cognition above all, and at least implicitly affirm the classical dictum of the French philosopher René Descartes (d. 1650): "I think, therefore I am." On the other hand, athletic phenoms such as Comăneci, Jordan, and Phelps suggest the transformation of that head-centered philosophy into "I perform, therefore I am."

It was only in the twentieth century that Western philosophers, such as Henri Bergson (d. 1941), began to seriously challenge Descartes' approach to knowing that focused on the head by moving the body more toward the center of the cognition process. In his groundbreaking *Matter and Memory: Essay on the Relationship of Body to Spirit*, Bergson spoke about the "intelligence of the body" (1988, 137), the "logic of the Body" (139), and what he called "bodily memory" (197). While Bergson's work has been critiqued—sometimes severely—over the ensuing decades, his concern to advocate this corporeal turn has been taken up by numerous other philosophers. Few have been as influential as Michel Foucault, who consistently argued for the primacy of doing over knowing, of practice over belief. Feminist scholars such as Susan Bordo (1989) have relied upon Foucault to illustrate how the various ways that women inhabit their bodies for good or for ill—Bordo gives particular attention to anorexia in her work—exhibit embodied way of knowing and being. Taking bodies individually and collectively as cultural texts, locations where power and politics are perceived and performed, is a necessary step toward shifting that power and rearranging those politics according to Bordo. Even a cautious philosopher such as Jesse Prinz—after surveying the current state of research on bodily cognition—concludes that "a complete theory of consciousness will be an embodied theory, in a moderate sense of the term" (2009, 434).

In a similar vein, reflective believing at the service of integrating may be best understood as a practice with its own ways of knowing. It is akin to the many other acts of care or leadership that chaplains and spiritual guides exercise when making a home visit, leading worship in mosque or synagogue, or organizing wellness checks on the homeless during extreme weather. While ministry requires systematic reflecting as its necessary companion, it is first and foremost a practice. In order to become proficient and effective in this practice, it is important to develop an embodied instinct, or what some call a *habitus*.

The French philosopher and sociologist Pierre Bourdieu (d. 2002) was a pioneer in thinking about the nature and power of habitus. Happily resonant with our previous reflections on Olympians, Bourdieu often discussed habitus in terms of sports, particularly through that refined athletic state he called "a feel for the game." He explains:

> Having the feel for the game is having the game under the skin; it is to master in a practical way the future of the game; it is to have a sense of history of the

game. While the bad player is always off tempo, always too early or too late, the good player is the one who *anticipates*, who is ahead of the game. Why can she get ahead of the flow of the game? Because she has the immanent tendencies of the game in her body, in an incorporated state: she embodies the game. (Bourdieu 1998, 80–81)

Such a refined instinct—or what Bourdieu also calls a "disposition"—belongs not only to the elite athlete but also to a wide range of practitioners who excel at their own "game." Consider emergency room personnel who instinctively launch into complicated medical procedures when faced with a gunshot victim, or that wise middle school teacher who can sense when the lesson plan is misfiring and quickly recalibrates the learning environment. It is also the gift of the seasoned spiritual guide who knows when to speak and when to be quiet while companioning a novice on their journey into enlightenment, or when sitting at the bedside of a friend in hospice.

Obviously developing such an expert feel for the game, whatever that game may be, takes a great deal of time and practice. Hubert and Stuart Dreyfus developed a useful framework for charting the arduous path to such proficiency by plotting out four preliminary "stages" through which one progresses on the way to the stage of expert (Dreyfus and Dreyfus 1986). In doing so they also signal the different sources of knowledge one employs to become a true expert (e.g., beginning with rules and theories and progressively moving to contextual understandings). They also inventively chart how one progresses in assessing data and decision making—for example, from applying information extracted from rules to intuitive action (see textbox 4.3).

While our immediate focus here is on orthopraxis, and the body knowledge required for reflective believing in service of and even symbolic of the integrating journey, the Dreyfus brothers' work still demonstrates that some theory, principles, and cognitive work is important, especially at the novice stages. While we will give more attention to this topic in the next part of this chapter, it seems important to note that body knowledge, intuition, and even habitus do not develop without reflection. Actually, Bourdieu is often criticized on this point because his understanding of habitus suggests that reflection is not required in the development of such dispositions. David Tracy is one eminent theologian who provides a useful counterpoint to Bourdieu. Not only does he reject the theory > practice model of doing theology so

CHARTING DREYFUS AND DREYFUS'S JOURNEY FROM NOVICE TO EXPERT

Stage	How Actions are Guided	Relationship between Knowing and Context	Orientation of Knowledge	Self-Investment in Process	Vision of Outcomes
Novice	Operates according to predetermined rules	Little reference to context	Knowledge is self-orientated	Detached from the process and its context	Only has outcomes for the moment
Advanced Beginner	Begins to move from rules to grasping underlying principles	Begins to recognize relevance of the context for understanding	Develops orientation toward the other (e.g., client) in resolving an issue for them	Developing some responsibility toward the other, but still quite detached	Outcomes envisioned for a single project
Competent Actor	Can adapt principles and guidelines to new situations	Discerns most significant parts of a situation contextually	Has acquired a vision of the wider field and its needs	A developed sense of responsibility, but often to one's own work arena or clients	Develops a vision of outcomes for home institution
Proficient Professional	Develops new principles and maxims in the face of unexpected events	Processes all understanding as essentially contextual	Thinks and acts systemically	Understands responsibility as extending system wide	Always thinks long term
Expert	Intuitive grasp of situations grounded in authentic wisdom	Is an instinctive contextual perceiver and responder	Intuitively understands that wisdom is for the common good	Intuits responsibility to humankind and the environment	Is instinctively visionary

Constructed from Dreyfus and Dreyfus 1986, 1–16; and Dreyfus 2004, especially 181.

prominent in much seminary training, he also rejects the practice > practice > practice model that Bourdieu seems to espouse. It is also a model unfortunately embodied in some very busy ministers, who make little time for reflection, and seem to hover continuously on the edge of burnout. According to Tracy, such an approach both negates theory and fails to recognize that all practice is, in fact, theory laden. Tracy's theological resolution—analogous to our thinking about integrating—is a practice > theory > practice approach that correlates theory and practice in a mutually critical kind of *perichoresis* (1983, 61–62).

Habitus not only requires a head check from time to time but also benefits from strong heart monitoring. Intuition and instinct can be very developed and highly refined but that does not mean they are always generative and just. As Bordo pointedly reminds us, since practice is a kind of skin technology—an action performed by and on both individual and collective bodies—it is also an exercise of power. This sometimes subtle, even hidden wielding of power can be for good or for ill. The abusive practices of spiritual and religious leaders—including those of my own tradition, too often in the headlines over the past decades—well document the potential for such abuse. The moral sensitivity characteristic of an authentically sacred heart and a vibrant orthokardia is a necessary balance in this affirmation of body knowledge and skin logic.

In particular, the orthokardiac gift of humility is singularly important for developing a habitus that respects the mind-boggling diversity of bodies in motion that dance through our current context. As a Caucasian academic raised in the "Ozzie and Harriett" world of the 1950s and ordained into a position of privilege, I constantly have to be careful not to impose uncritically the presumptions from my own context and worldview on those of others. Teaching and leading worship in a multicultural, cross-contextual environment over three decades has been especially informative and sometimes chastening for me in this regard. I began my ministry of presiding and preaching in a post–Vatican II church, eager for the participation and engagement of worshippers—particularly the young. Early years as a campus minister at an all-women's college in Minnesota in the late 1970s offered an environment in which I came to believe that being energetic, relevant, and even entertaining was the key to leading effective worship.

In my early years of instructing others to preside, I tried to imprint my body knowledge upon the bodies of my students: women and men from

around the globe. "Keep your chin up . . . look into the eyes of the assembly . . .
use your whole body when you give the embrace of peace." Yet students from
Thailand did not throw their torsos into the sign of peace, and instead slowly
bowed toward each other with folded hands. Japanese students informed
me that looking directly into the eyes of another, especially an elder, could
be a sign of disrespect. Vietnamese students—some of whom had begun
their ministry studies before the fall of Saigon, spent decades as refugees and
sojourners, and were completing their studies after more than a thirty-year
journey—reminded me that worship was no laughing matter. Then there
were the women students who pointed out that they made a prayer gesture
with their arms different from mine because they were shaped differently
than I was. Ouch!

Reflective believing in the service of the integrating journey is embodied
believing. Like an athlete, the reflective believer disciplines the body so that its
movement contributes to harmony instead of discord. For those who practice
Prāṇāyām, this means learning to harness one's breathing. For those who follow
the Prophet Mohammed, who fasted two days each week, this means fasting
from food and water frequently and especially keeping the holy fast of Ramadan. For those who observe some monastic way, this often translates into keeping vigils and observing long hours of prayer during the night. Others discipline
the body through modesty of dress, simplicity in food, and abstention from
certain beverages. In our rhizomatic worldview, there is no singular way of engaging in such discipline effectively. Yet engage we must if we are to acquire not
only body knowledge but also body wisdom in service of reflective believing.

THINKING IS A PRACTICE, TOO

This final turn to orthodoxy or "right thinking" is not intended in any way
to diminish the importance of seriously engaging all of our cognitive pow-
ers in reflective believing. Rather, it is meant to balance or even subvert the
privileged authority that theoretical work is often given in training people in
the practices of ministry. To use the arboreal image from chapter 1, theory is
not the taproot, from which all wisdom sprouts. Rather, it is part of the rhizomatic formula, a necessary element in an integrating *perichoresis*, one leg of
the three-legged stool that offers balance to the juggling act we call ministry.
The story at the beginning of this chapter of my somewhat disastrous organ
jury underscored for me the importance of systematic study for an immature

musician who was making music at the surface level with little depth perception of the underpinnings of this "theory-laden" practice. Theory and critical thinking are important, as capsulated in the pithy wisdom of a revered professor. In response to a seminarian's impatience with the challenging concepts from an advanced course in systematic theology, and eager to have "real experiences" in ministry, our professor replied, "reading is also a real experience."

One's Own Heritage

A crucial, if not first, step for "right thinking" in reflecting across the myriad forms of believing that mark today's landscape is acquiring fluency with one's own foundations for believing. It may be tempting to plunge into what could appear as the exotic way others believe. However, without solid moorings in the traditions that give rise to my own way of believing, I am potentially a less effective dialogue partner for others. In all honesty, it is difficult to be a sounding board for other ways of believing if my own believing framework is insubstantial. Think back, for example, on Katherine and Fareed from chapter 3. As they launch into their interfaith marriage, they become the first interpreters of their inherited belief systems for both their spouse and their children. If one spouse or parent is notably more fluent in their home tradition than another, the dialogue between Islam and Roman Catholicism in their household and emerging family will be proportionately impaired. An ancient legal adage states *Nemo potest dare quod non habet*, roughly translated as "you can't give what you haven't got." It is useful wisdom to keep in mind when questioning the legality of any sale or purchase (its original context), as well as when thinking about entering the crucible of reflective believing.

One of the kernels of wisdom in James and Evelyn Whitehead's design of their tripartite model for theological reflection (see appendix 1D) is not only the integral role for tradition as a dialogue partner but also the exhortation for reflectors to "befriend" that tradition. Admittedly, their definition of tradition is quite restricted, limited to explicitly religious traditions and, even more narrowly, to the Christian tradition alone. Even with that caveat, however, they are still on to something exceedingly vital in the reflective arts. In their experience they found that the Roman Catholic seminarians they were supervising were often more adept at social analysis than they were at befriending their own religious heritage as a resource for pastoral decision making. That has often been my experience as well. *Nemo potest dare quod non habet.*

I would dare to venture that the challenge to find solid moorings in one's heritage is not simply a challenge for those of us who belong to the Abrahamic religions, other theists, Buddhists, or Jainists, but even for humanists. In my reading of and interview with self-admitted atheist Chris Stedman, for example, I was surprised and delighted to find him talking about his need to develop his own "canon" (Stedman 2012, 82). He writes about how he had "faltered when discerning how to identify" himself (136), his need to "devour Humanist literature," and his journey into embracing a humanist worldview that was something he "needed to act upon" (137). He also mused in an interview about the challenge of building a humanist community with positive goals and grounded in some common moorings, since so often humanists are clearer about what they are against rather than what they are for. Thus, whether it is identified as a religious tradition, spiritual inheritance, humanist canon, or some other designation, we render both our dialogue partners and ourselves a great service by having fluency in and critically thinking about the inherited wisdom that anchors us.

Some forms of believing might rightfully resist any image of being "anchored" in a particular tradition. Such language could intimate that believing is essentially the defense of an immutable bedrock of prepackaged ideas rather than a path leading to enlightenment. It is a struggle many have with my own tradition. Roman Catholicism has many dogmatically defined beliefs and teachings, as well as countless authoritative instructions from popes and bishops and innumerable other leaders or agencies. At the same time, however, those who self-identify as Roman Catholics vary greatly in their acceptance or rejection of many such teachings (Univision 2014).

One of the liberating things about having spent decades "befriending" my tradition, as the Whiteheads would have it, is knowing that the vast and pluriform tradition blithely labeled "Roman Catholic" is not a stolid citadel of uniform beliefs but a multicontextual tapestry that expresses myriad modes of believing. While often presented as a single-lane highway, with high tolls that rigidly control its entry and a horde of police—ordained and otherwise—prepared to eject any deviant believers from that Catholic highway, my beloved church is much more complex and forgiving than that. A fresh symbol of this complexity and hospitality was Pope Francis's willingness to officiate publicly at the marriage of twenty couples in September 2014, some of whom were cohabitating while others already had children. This is the same shepherd who preached that heaven is not just a place for Catholics, or even Christians, but also one for all who do good—even atheists (Huffington Post, 2013)!

Christianity has an ancient image reaching back into at least the third century CE of the church as a boat—sometimes called the "Bark of Peter." It recognizes the Christian journey as a fluid and sometime dangerous passage that a community makes with a steady leader at the helm. One of the most famous Buddhist parables is similarly about a raft that is an important vehicle for getting people to the shore. While the raft (a metaphor for the *Dharma*) is not to be held onto, it needs to be sturdy enough to weather the storms and get us to our destination (see textbox 4.4).

TEXTBOX 4.4

A man is trapped on one side of a fast-flowing river. Where he stands, there is great danger and uncertainty—but on the far side of the river, there is safety. But there is no bridge or ferry for crossing. So the man gathers logs, leaves, twigs, and vines and is able to fashion a raft sturdy enough to carry him to the other shore. By lying on the raft and using his arms to paddle, he crosses the river to safety.

The Buddha then asked the listeners a question: "What would you think if the man, having crossed over the river, then said to himself, 'Oh, this raft has served me so well, I should strap it on to my back and carry it over land now?'"

The monks replied that it would not be very sensible to cling to the raft in such a way.

The Buddha continues: "What if he lay the raft down gratefully, thinking that this raft has served him well, but is no longer of use, and can thus be laid down upon the shore?"

The monks replied that this would be the proper attitude.

The Buddha concluded by saying, "So it is with my teachings, which are like a raft, and are for crossing over with—not for seizing hold of."

On this spiritual ocean, those of us willing to ride such currents of believing can still have anchors, but maybe something more akin to a "sea anchor" than a forged iron instrument of enormous weight and strength that locks us to some magisterial substratum, preventing us from drifting away. Traditional anchors—sometimes akin to arboreal understandings of belief—secure a vessel in a single place. Sea anchors, on the other hand, are only tethered to the ship and not to the sea floor. Designed to establish as much drag as possible in the water, they serve as both a kind of stabilizer and a gentle brake.

Critical thinking about our own moorings or "sea anchors" is one of the ways to assess the worthiness of our raft, particularly as a vehicle for the dialogue of reflective believing. As Stephen Brookfield (2012) explains, critical thinking—a clarifying synonym for "orthodoxy"—is not the same thing as acquiring information. Computers are filled with information, but the great challenge for those who work in artificial intelligence is getting super computers to translate information into critical reasoning. For Brookfield, critical reasoning presumes acquiring what he calls the *grammar of a subject*, or those building blocks of knowledge that every student of that subject needs to know in order to be regarded as well versed in it (Brookfield 2012, 28). In light of that body of information, critical thinking involves (1) discovering what assumptions we and others hold, (2) checking to see how much sense those assumptions make (3) by trying to look at them from multiple viewpoints (4) for the sake of taking informed actions that are grounded in the evidence, can be explained to others, and have a good chance of achieving the desired results (Brookfield 2012, 24).

This kind of "right" thinking is obviously not blind adherence to whatever heritage we claim. Nor is it an apologetic stance armed with a sophisticated defense of every thread and fiber of that heritage. Rather, this is right thinking done with a sacred heart: an appreciative consideration of the heritage we embrace employing critical skills so that our embrace might be more enlightened, life-giving, and cause for action.

Other Ways of Believing

Besides acquiring the grammar of our own "sea anchor" or heritage, right thinking in service of reflective believing also requires that we develop some knowledge about the ways that others believe. Eboo Patel, founder of the Interfaith Youth Core, employs a useful term for this project: *interfaith literacy.*

For Patel, interfaith literacy, which he considers "an appreciative knowledge of other traditions" (2012, 95), has four different stages. First, Patel believes it means learning about what we admire in other faiths (e.g., the beauty of their texts and the contributions of their adherents to society). Stage two is an ability to identify values that all religions share. Third is having an understanding of the history of interfaith cooperation. Last is developing one's own theology of interfaith cooperation rooted in your own tradition (2012, 95–99). As with our consideration of "integrating," this is an enduring life-long journey.

Employing the categories of the Dreyfus brothers, the task for novices is to acquire information, or what Brookfield calls the *grammar of a subject*. It seems ordinarily inappropriate and probably an act of hubris for some outsider like myself to launch into critical thinking about another tradition without first acquiring a solid and cohesive body of information about another spiritual heritage or canon of beliefs. Sometimes this process demands acquiring certain language skills, for example, in order to perceive something of the rich poetry and lyrical nature of the Qur'an, which is only prayed in Arabic. Even when we have acquired some proficiencies in language and information, most of us seldom move beyond the stage of an advanced beginner, and few acquire competency, much less proficiency, in another way of believing. Thus it is ordinarily best that we leave the critical thinking about other traditions— especially as it comprises the testing of the assumptions that undergird such believing—to the adherents of those traditions.

That does not mean, however, that we abandon critical thinking when encountering the believing patterns of another. Brookfield believes that the essence of critical thinking is hunting down our assumptions. That can be an enormously beneficial exercise *if* it is focused on our own assumptions about other ways of believing. This exercise might also be enhanced by employing what Wes Jackson has called an "ignorance-based worldview." A botanist and geneticist, Jackson is president of the Land Institute, concerned with the establishment of agricultural patterns that are ecologically sustainable and productive. As a scientist, he and his collaborators are concerned that too often decisions about land and ecology are made by people with insufficient information who nonetheless forge ahead, sometimes causing more harm than good to the environment. In preparation for a 2004 conference on an "ignorance-based worldview," he extended an invitation that mused, "Imagine an ignorance-based science and technology in which practitioners would be ever conscious that we are billions of times more ignorant than knowledgeable and always will be" (Jackson 2005).

That caution in the face of ecological issues and land science is most appropriate for us as we ponder the mystery of believing, especially the believing of another. Exploring our assumptions about believing in appreciate mode also requires that orthokardiac gift of humility. The ways that others engage in believing is "holy ground." This respect is enhanced by an "ignorance-based" approach—or maybe better a "humility-based" approach—which assumes that, as outsiders, we really know very little if anything of substance about another's way of believing. What we might have seen on the news or on the Internet is seldom a sure guide into the heart of another's believing. Furthermore, there is such pluriformity under the broad umbrellas of humanism, Buddhism, or Islam that to generalize is to wager on being at least inaccurate, if not outright wrong. In my own tradition, there are currently well over 1.2 billion Roman Catholics in the world. The diversity of beliefs across that spectrum—not to mention the diversity of beliefs just across my own extended family—requires nuance and respect rather than glib generalization. The pluriformity of my own tradition is mind-boggling. Thus, when I hear someone—especially a graduate student at my own institution—begin a sentence with "The church has always taught that . . ." I give them about a 5 percent chance of being correct.

Critical thinking in the service of reflective believing always needs to travel with its other two siblings: a right heart and attuned embodiment. For the novice, this often means following the ancient advice of Hippocrates: "Do no harm." In the face of mystery, we are always novices and thus in the juggling of head, hand, and heart we must tread gently on this holy ground.

A POSTSCRIPT

Some of my colleagues encouraged me to offer this postscript related to my experience of the organ jury narrated at the beginning of this chapter. In that formative event a wise organ professor, who discovered that I had never studied music theory, commented, "You'll play better after you've had some theory." Almost twenty-five years after that experience, I was invited back to that same university and offered a lecture on spiritual acoustics titled "Sound Theology." As part of that lecture I repeated the story, underscoring that it was people from that place of learning who had encouraged and prodded me to wed my performing with good theory, and done so in such a caring way. After the lecture, a graying gentleman came up to me, shook my hand, and said, "I see you've learned some theory since then." It was the same professor, the same wise guide who encouraged intelligent performing, and did so with a sacred heart. The journey continues.

Some Assembly Required

To dare is to lose one's footing momentarily. Not to dare is to lose oneself.

—*attributed to Søren Kierkegaard*

A favorite Christmas story from our family folklore—appropriately embellished over the decades—surrounds the wishes of a younger sister to have Santa Claus bring her a Barbie dollhouse. While of limited means, my parents struggled mightily to make each Christmas memorable as they attempted to fulfill and often anticipate the usually modest wishes of their children. That year they located the desired object in one of those reference-size print catalogs that often showed up at our doorstep, and Dad dutifully drove to Sears & Roebuck to pick it up. As I was of a post–Santa Claus age at the time, I was in on the plot and remember Dad bringing in this large, flat box that they hid in their bedroom. Since Santa Claus only showed up at our house when children were asleep, my parents hauled out the box after my younger siblings were tucked away on Christmas Eve. While Dad presumed that the dollhouse would have to be put together, neither he nor Mom were prepared for the byzantine directions and hundreds of maneuvers necessary for constructing this highly anticipated gift. Fabricated of heavy cardboard, the pieces of the miniature dwelling were fitted together according to a "tab" and "slot" design. Mom read out the directions while Dad (an industrial engineer) would try to figure out where "tab G" was and how it fit into "slot G." It was a night of mounting frustration as they labored into the wee hours of the morning, desperate to finish the present before my younger siblings would bolt out of their rooms at the crack of dawn. To this day the phrase "some assembly required" strikes fear into the hearts of many of my family members.

In the previous chapters we have tried to sketch something of the promises and challenges of reimagining theological reflection at this era of mind-boggling diversity in ways of believing. To that end we addressed issues of language and possible modes of engaging in what we are calling reflective believing. This also involved our exploring the multiple and sometimes contradictory purposes this reimagined form of theological reflection can serve, as well as considering a few of the many contexts in which it may be practiced. As an exercise that both models and contributes to the integrating process, we more recently examined the juggling of orthodoxy, orthopraxis, and orthopathy and the necessity of connecting head, hand, and heart for effective reflective believing and the integrating trajectory that I believe it needs to nourish.

Given that journey, we are finally positioned to define reflective believing as a meaning-making practice, exercised in light of one's individual or shared wisdom-heritage, that honors the experiences and stories of its participants. Employed for diverse purposes, it welcomes and displays a holy envy for other ways of believing, while recognizing the bond of humanity between all participants. Necessarily improvisational, it displays respect for the common good and exercises humility in knowing how to contribute to that good.

This language game is not conceived as a new method designed to replace previously imagined models of TR. Rather, it is a more liquid approach to meaning making constructed around a series of presuppositions or, à la Wittgenstein, a set of rules for playing the game. We can now enumerate some of those rules for RB, recognizing that—as in Wittgenstein—the numbering does not necessarily mirror the priority or value of a rule.

1. RB is *not theistic* at its core but is a language game that can be played by both theists and nontheists.
2. RB does *not supplant TR*, which continues to be useful in many circles.
3. While indebted to TR, RB is a *different language game* particularly because of its willingness to engage both theists and nontheists in reflecting together.
4. RB is a form of *meaning making*, and at its core is an interpretive or hermeneutical event.

5. Shared *humanity* is common ground for entering this game.
6. There is *no single method* for engaging in RB.
7. Like many art forms, RB requires *improvisation*.
8. There is *no single starting point* for engaging in RB.
9. *Experiences* of believing and the *narrating* of those experiences are common and valued elements in RB.
10. Participants in RB are invited to explore and "befriend" their own humanist, spiritual, or religious *heritages and traditions*.
11. While RB can be an individual activity, it is envisioned as a *shared experience*, often engaging unexpected dialogue partners.
12. RB first *honors difference* rather than questioning it.
13. While intention is important, *RB is a practice* not simply an idea.
14. Its performance is enhanced when its players exhibit certain *characteristics or virtues*, especially
    a. *respect* and *even awe* when invited into another's way of believing;
    b. *humility* in the face of what cannot easily be explained;
    c. *courage* when encountering forms of believing that challenge one's own;
    d. a sense of *peacefulness* that disallows one to move too quickly to judging; and
    e. a *holy envy* that looks for beauty in other ways of believing.
15. *Listening* is an important skill for effective RB.
16. There are *multiple "languages"* that can be employed in RB, including
    a. body language;
    b. silence;
    c. ritualizing; and
    d. storytelling.
17. RB can be employed in the services of a *wide range of goals*.
18. The purpose for which one engages in RB should *influence the methods* one employs for doing so.
19. RB contributes to establishing and maintaining an *integrating trajectory* for both individuals and communities.
20. RB invites a *balance* between what is known with the head and through the body with deep feelings or heart knowledge.
21. RB exhibits a *moral sensitivity* that seeks the potential for good that resides in every human heart.

22. Beginners in RB ordinarily benefit greatly from a *mentor or guide* to lead them into this reflective path.
23. For the mature reflective believer, this *art becomes a habitus* (Foley 2014, 71–72).

Given these rules or grammatical guides to RB, it might seem appropriate at long last to reveal the heretofore hidden ideal formula and exact steps for actually engaging in reflective believing. Unfortunately, not only is that impossible, but it would also be an act of untempered hubris. While I have shared perspectives and experiences about various aspects of RB, even outlining a grammar for effective reflective believing, there is no "tab A into slot A" design that even comes close to universal applicability. There are simply too many variables in this dynamic environment. That is why already in chapter 2 I suggested that engagement in chaplaincy, ministry, or other forms of spiritual service requires an improvisational discipline and spirit (reiterated in rule no. 7 above) that cannot be limited to a single model or method of doing TR. Admittedly, I have talked about "mapping" some of the contours of reflective believing, yet all mapping is flawed. Timothy Ferris highlights that reality when he speaks about the "sadness of maps." This sadness or imperfection occurs because maps contain less information than the territory they are trying to represent and because they introduce distortions (Ferris 2005, 70–71). One of my favorite images of such distorting is the celebrated cover of the *New Yorker* from 1976 by Saul Steinberg, which provides an intentionally jaundiced and iconic view of the world from 9th Avenue in New York (Steinberg 1976). As someone who has spent much of his life in or around Chicago, this "Big Apple" perspective is both amusing and unsettling to us inhabitants of the "Second City."

While we did not have Ferris's language in 1988 when we began designing our Ecumenical Doctor of Ministry degree, we nonetheless intuited early on in that process the inadequacy of the ways we were mapping theological reflection. Our students were from around the world, experienced in contexts and situations that the faculty leading the program would never experience much less fully understand from a distance. As the diversity of Christians who matriculated into the program expanded, and then Muslims gifted us with their presence, the sadness of our mapping was multiplied. How does a middle-aged, Caucasian, Western-educated, Roman Catholic cleric from urban middle America, for example, teach advanced ministry skills to a much younger female Korean Presbyterian pastor who is doubtful that her church will even allow her into leadership when she returns to her country of origin? Our solution to this dilemma was to focus on teaching methods. We did so by exposing these experienced leaders to a vast array of methods, in effect, to the way that others had "played the game" of TR around the globe and in varying contexts. By inviting students to both commend what was useful in those various approaches and respectfully critique what they perceived to be problematic from the vantage point of their own contexts, we hoped and expected that they would be in a position to construct their own contextually credible methods for leading and teaching theological reflection. Presenting their own reconceived method for TR was actually the first major gatekeeping event in that program. Some assembly required!

In many respects this volume is hoping to achieve something similar for you, the reader. By exposing you to some of the building blocks and obstacles, perspectives and pitfalls, particular to the language game of reflective believing, you are invited not only to consider the ways that I am reimagining theological reflection but also to do your *own reimagining*. Some assembly is required! Furthermore, as different believers are at different stages in this journey of learning, deconstructing, and reimagining TR, it does not seem wise to presume that everyone engages in this reimagining or reconstruction in the same way. Cognizant of the fact that some readers are beginners in this process and others are very experienced mentors in the reflecting arts, we will return to the work of the Dreyfus brothers introduced in the previous chapter and their inventive framework for thinking about the path to proficiency from novice to expert in this reimagining process.

OF META-PRINCIPLES AND INDIAN STEW

Before returning to the framework of the Dreyfus brothers, however, it seems useful to offer one excursus on a key strategic contribution of James and Evelyn Whitehead. As related in the opening chapter, my ever-widening exposure to experienced ministers from different contexts and varying ways of believing has moved me to abandon my sole reliance on their method or any single method for theological reflection. At the same time, however, I consistently find the distinction that the Whiteheads make between a model and a method in this reflective process enormously useful, especially if you are engaged in the constructive work that I am proposing for contemporary reflective believers.

As outlined in appendix 1D, the Whiteheads conceived their ground-breaking approach to theological reflection by juxtaposing three dialogue partners or components that comprise their "model" with a three-stage movement that defines the "method" element in their process. The use of "models" as a form of reasoning is well known to scientists of many stripes. Cognitive scientist Nancy Nersessian argues, however, that beyond the sciences, *model-based reasoning* is a fundamental form of human thinking and is employed by people across a spectrum of problem solving exercise, from the quite mundane—like figuring out how to get a chair through a doorway (see figure 5.1)—to more esoteric problems in astrophysics or genetics (Nersessian 1999, 14). Western theologies explicitly began to borrow the language

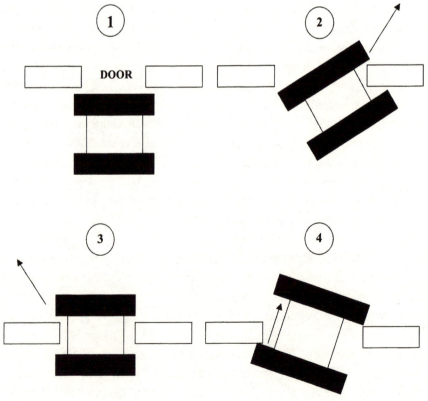

FIGURE 5.1.

and concept of "models" as a style of inquiry in the 1960s. One of the more influential works in this regard was that of Roman Catholic theologian Avery Dulles, who in 1974 published his very popular *Models of the Church*.

Ordinarily models include not only elements or nouns like chairs and doors but also the verbs for negotiating the chair through the particular doorway that looms on the horizon as the primary obstacle to be overcome. What the Whiteheads have done in order to render their approach both rich and accessible is, in a sense, to separate out the nouns from the verbs in their process. Thus their model is delimited to the elements (i.e., nouns) that one should engage when pursuing theological reflection according to their design. Accordingly, they cast their process in the image of a dialogue—a popular metaphor in contemporary hermeneutics—and their model outlines the essential dialogue partners or sources of information that must be engaged in their form of TR.

While I have indicated some of my critique of the dialogue partners the Whiteheads put forward (see appendix 1D), what their particular approach to their model underscores in a simple and clarifying way is the importance of multiple resources or dialogue partners, no matter how you select or configure them. Notice the emphasis is on *partners*. A dialogue only with your experience, for example, is really not a dialogue. Intuiting the need for dialogue partners outside myself seems to be an act of basic common sense. The Whiteheads themselves caution that their proposed process fails if you only listen to one source of information (Whitehead and Whitehead 1995, 83). There is also some empirical evidence of the importance of clear and multiple dialogue partners in whatever form of reimagined TR you construct. In 2006, Thomas O'Connor and Elizabeth Meakes conducted a study in order to discover what sources for theological reflection were being employed by professionals engaged in pastoral care and counseling in Canada. Their study "verifies" the importance of multiple sources among their relatively large sample of interviewees (O'Connor and Meakes 2008, 123). It also clarifies that all sources are *not* of equal weight among these practitioners. This might suggest that not only does one need multiple sources for a process of reflective believing, but it is also valuable to weigh those sources so one is self-aware of how they (or others) may instinctively privilege one source over another in the dialogue. The interviewees in O'Connor and Meakes's study, for example, rated sacred texts—including Jewish and Christian scriptures, the Qur'an,

Buddhist and Hindu writings—as the most important source in their work of theological reflection.

While the conceptual framework of the Whiteheads gathers all of the resources for dialogue (the "nouns") under the rubric of their "model," they outline the rules for conducting that dialogue (the "verbs") under the framework of their "method." They themselves have nuanced those rules in the second edition of their influential work, and changed them from *attending-asserting-deciding* to *attending-asserting-pastoral response*: a fine illustration of how even celebrated mentors keep improvising. While one can agree or disagree with some or all of their rules or progression for this reflective conversation—and I both agree and disagree with some aspects of their process—what does not seem dismissible is the necessity of having some rules or progression for entering the game of reflective believing. RB is not simply about having beliefs or a heritage, personal opinions or some understanding of one's context. It is doing something with those for a purpose, whether that purpose is personal enlightenment or pastoral problem solving. Furthermore, such purposes extend beyond ourselves, a point we previously made explicit in chapter 2 when first suggesting that the game of RB requires "watching our language in the presence of others." Having what Wittgenstein would consider "rules for the game" is critical for the process to advance in constructive and respectful ways in the presence of those honored others.

Framing reflective believing as a type of conversation, in which there are both dialogue partners (i.e., the people in the conversation as well as the resources upon which they rely), plus some rules for how the dialogue proceeds, could be considered a kind of metaprinciple or overarching grammatical rule for crafting this game. One of the contributions of this metaprinciple is that, beyond positioning us to be attentive to what voices are sitting around the metaphorical table of RB and how they are being heard, it also prods us to ask "Who is missing?" or "Who is not speaking or being heard?" This is not to suggest that every possible resource for this reimagined theological reflection has to be operative in every experience of RB. That is not humanly possible or even useful. Nonetheless, participants and especially any leadership in this enterprise should be alerted to whom or what is missing from the event and how such absences impact the process in sometimes subtle but nonetheless real ways. In some respects, one of the incentives for the Whiteheads to give "tradition" such a prominent role in their tripartite model was precisely because the seminarians they were supervising in field education were not inclined to engage their own religious tradition in the process of pastoral decision making.

A second contribution of this metaprinciple is its inference that effective RB presumes that all of the voices somehow interact with each other. The Whiteheads addressed this necessity in their framework in the step with the admittedly challenging name "the assertion stage": language that they themselves experienced as problematic for their students during their many years teaching at universities in mainland China. In some spiritual traditions this stage or process is understood as one of discerning. Some contemporary religious thinkers prefer the language of "correlation," or what David Tracy emphasizes should be a "mutual critical correlation" (1983, 61–62). As suggested by one student many years ago, a more savory metaphor for this interface process that might be more appealing to a broad array of folk is borrowed from the world of cooking (i.e., making stew!).

There are people in many contexts who create some form of stew in which various elements are slowly cooked together in some liquid usually over a low heat. In the northern regions of India, Pakistan, and Bangladesh, for example, *nihari* is quite popular, especially as the weather cools. It combines beef or lamb, onions, garlic, ginger, cinnamon, cilantro, and other spices—the cook often throwing in whatever seasonings are at hand—slowly steeping over a low flame or embers. The goal in this and other stews is not to destroy the individual ingredients and turn the food to some lump of indistinguishable elements mashed together in a culinary mystery, but to allow the various elements slowly to take on the tastes and nuances of the others, rendering a medley of distinctive yet harmonious tastes in the final dish. Reflective believing is an analogous event, in which the various voices and resources, welcomed into an environment of respect and holy envy, slowly acquire an appreciative taste for the other without sacrificing the distinctiveness of their own heritages or perspectives.

Having some constellation of nouns and verbs—whether imagined as dialogue partners and ground rules for the conversation, or food stuffs and the process for transforming them into a feast—is one of my basic metaprinciples when shaping frameworks for effective reflective believing. Moreover, novices on this journey are often aided when the framework at hand clearly distinguishes the voices from the progression that those voices might follow, as in the Whiteheads' "model" and "method." This is one of the reasons that I am cautious about employing the method developed by the Belgian Joseph Cardijn (d. 1967) known as "see-judge-act" (Cardijn 1914), especially with beginners. It is true that this method has been widely and effectively used, first by members of the organization of Young Christian Workers that Cardijn founded, and later by many who discovered its liberative potential at the grassroots level, particularly in South America. Those contexts, however, often presumed implicit and sometimes invariable dialogue partners such as the Christian scriptures and Roman Catholic social teaching. As a process for theological reflection in other contexts, however, it has no such implicit "model" or designated resources upon which to draw, but only a "method" or process for proceeding. It clearly directs the participant "to see" but does not specify what sources to look at. Then one is to judge, but again with no specific criteria for making such a judgment. Reimagined forms of reflective believing are better served when both the nouns and the verbs—the metaphorical food stuffs and the process for transforming them into a feast—have some clarity about them.

THE DREYFUS BROTHERS REDUX

In chapter 4 we first referenced the influential work of Hubert and Stuart Dreyfus, whose research led them to create a model that charts the progression for acquiring certain performance skills over time. Their original investigation (Dreyfus and Dreyfus 1980), carried out under contract with the United States Air Force, was designed to analyze how jet pilots became experts at their craft. This was done in order to help develop step-by-step training strategies that would consistently produce pilots with such expertise. The schema that eventually emerged from this research, refined in their later publications (Dreyfus and Dreyfus 1986, 1–16), posited five different stages in the acquisition of such skills: (1) novice, (2) advanced beginner, (3) competent actor, (4) proficient professional, and (5) expert.

The growing influence of the Dreyfus brothers' model over the last few decades is evident in the ways it has shaped many forms of professional education from ministry to the medical fields. Any model this influential—akin to the "classic" models of TR outlined in the appendixes of this book—will undergo brisk review and a fair amount of critique. For example, one thought-provoking review by Dr. Adolfo Peña, a specialist in surgical and acute medical care, finds their approach highly problematic for training physicians. Among the critiques he cites are its linear vision of learning, its lack of attention to social structures and social knowledge, and particularly because moving toward the expert stage seems to suggest increased and ultimately sole reliance upon intuition while disregarding the role of explicit knowledge and the consistent need for acquiring such knowledge in practicing the medical arts (2010).

Peña's considered critique, along with that of others that he well summarizes, suggests that we employ the model of the Dreyfus brothers here with due caution. Thus it is decidedly not proposed as some type of proficiency ladder that one can climb, carefully stepping from one rung to another until finally achieving the ultimate goal of expert or certified guru. Anyone who has ever embarked on a spiritual journey or attempted a trek into the transcendent understands that this is a twisting path that often doubles back on itself, is filled with dead ends, and seldom, if ever, arrives at some Mt. Everest. At the same time, there is accumulated wisdom that can be effectively employed to map out some of the contours of the journey and can lead us to high ground. With due caution we also recall Timothy Ferris's concern about the sadness of maps with their necessary elimination and distortion. We explore the Dreyfus brothers' model here as such a helpful yet distorted framework. Maps like frameworks are distinctive from the realities to which they point, and need to be treated as such.

The Novice

All of us have had experiences of being a complete beginner at something, although quite often we were incapable or unprepared for being reflective about our rookie status at the time. Childhood in many respects is the original "amateur hour" in which we are neophytes at virtually every fundamental human capacity including talking, eating, and walking. The amusing results of our learning attempts with such fundamentals are the stuff of baby books and family legends. Our apprenticeship at life continues for decades, and adolescence could be imagined as that extended period of our development in which we consistently encounter the new, which radically changes us on a regular basis. As we grow older we certainly continue to experience things that radically change us, but it is increasingly less and less a pattern.

In my own life, not only have I been a greenhorn at walking and riding a bike, learning a language, and writing a research paper, I was also literally a "novice" when I joined my religious community at the ripe old age of seventeen. The ritual that technically rendered one a member of my religious community was the rite of investiture in which the initiate for the first time is clothed in the long brown robe characteristic of many of those who followed Francis of Assisi as a patron and spiritual guide. I have a distinctive memory on the day of investiture, having donned that brown robe for the first time, thinking to myself, "I'm a Franciscan!" I look back on that moment with some embarrassment, only relieved that I don't think I said it aloud for others to hear. It is true that I might have looked like a Franciscan on the outside, but in all other respects I was a complete newbie when it came to religious life.

Over the next nine years of initial formation, I learned the rules, including literally being required to memorize the Rule of St. Francis in all its happy brevity. Besides the head knowledge, entering into this life also necessitated shaping a different heart and shaping a place in my deep affections for sometimes complete strangers who shared the same heritage and were now my brothers. It also demanded new forms of embodiment, such as how to walk down a staircase in a long robe and sandals without tripping or how to drop to your knees and kiss the floor when entering the chapel with some grace and without falling flat on your face. It took me almost the entire novitiate year for my body to figure out the aerodynamics of those moves. The mind and body, but especially the heart, are still under construction.

As the Dreyfus brothers point out, novices need a lot of information and helpful rules for figuring out what to do with that information. It does not mean, however, that they are completely devoid of knowledge or even relevant experiences and must operate like little robots programmed by whatever data their instructors can stuff inside their empty heads. As some critics of the Dreyfus brothers' schema remind us, novices have both knowledge and experience. What they often have even more of is a good heart and plenty of orthokardia to offset their often underdeveloped orthodoxy and orthopraxis. At its root meaning, an amateur is someone who loves (*amo* in Latin). When it comes to reflective believing, motivated by such love, a primary task for the beginner is to start the long process of bringing head-hand-heart into an initial equilibrium. While many amateurs instinctively lead with the heart, moving toward a first integrating stage in reflective believing also seems to require first learning and then robustly exercising some previously devised and tested form of theological reflection.

The appendixes to this volume contain brief introductions to and assessments of four well-established and widely practiced forms of theological reflection: (1) Thomas Groome's "shared praxis," (2) Joe Holland and Peter Henriot's "pastoral circle," (3) Patricia O'Connell Killen and John de Beer's "meaning making" process, and (4) James and Evelyn Whitehead's "model and method" approach. I have also included a new variation on TR, designed by former student and now colleague Christina Zaker. While there are significant similarities between these approaches, and even reliance upon each other or similar sources, each was conceived for a slightly different purpose and context. Groome's work, influenced by the liberationist theories of Paulo Freire, evolved as a new path for doing religious education. Holland and Henriot were influenced by the previously mentioned work of Joseph Cardijn, but also by more sophisticated liberationists and their approaches for responding to social problems, especially as experienced by the oppressed in the southern hemisphere. Killen and de Beer's work might be best understood as one that is fundamentally concerned with the pursuit of wisdom and personal meaning making. The Whiteheads' work, on the other hand, is more adept at enabling one to make informed pastoral decisions and respond to particular ministerial dilemmas. Zaker's nuancing of TR was a result of what she saw to be a need for a more biblical approach to the reflective arts.

The novice might begin by first reading through the brief synopses that I have provided of these "classical" approaches to TR. In doing so, be conscious of what elements or moves in them are resonant with your own personal preferences and tastes as you imagine both exercising and even eventually constructing your own process for reflective believing. Besides personal inclinations, however, try to attend to the intended and primary purposes for your engaging in this reflective exercise. Like any instrument you choose, the method you employ does have an effect on the outcome. Oil painting with a palette knife is certainly possible, and celebrated artists such as Vincent van Gogh (d. 1890) did so with great effect. If, however, your goal is painting in the pointillist style of George Seurat (d. 1891), as exemplified in his famous *A Sunday Afternoon on La Grand Jatte*, the palette knife is probably not your best choice. Similarly, if reflection in the service of some liberative action is the primary purpose of your reflective work, then the processes of Killen and de Beer or the Whiteheads might not be as helpful as that of Holland and Henriot.

Once you've selected a classic model, approach it with a Krister Stendahl heart filled with holy envy rather than the exacting eye of a professional art critic. Of course, there are going to be limitations and problems with whatever method you choose. As noted from the outset of this enterprise, that is a fundamental reason for the very writing of this book. However, it seems difficult to provide an adequate critique or even position yourself to move beyond some classical form of TR on your way to reflectively believing without having first thoroughly exercised some well-tested model. That probably will dictate reading beyond the sketches provided here, and delving into some, if not all, of the original exposé of the methods as presented by their originators.

It is probable that even at this beginning level it will be necessary for some to make a few basic substitutions in whatever method you employ. If you are a Sikh, for example, and you were drawn to employ Groome's shared praxis model, instead of having a dialogue with the Christian scriptures as suggested in his third step, you might naturally turn to the *Guru Granth Sahib*. If you are a humanist, you might have to begin—à la Chris Stedman—by constructing your own "canon" that can ground you in some deep part of your believing heritage and allow you to exercise Groome's method with some integrity. These substitutions allow you to respect the basic thrust and design of the original model while rendering it palatable to your own mode of believing. It will also position you to be a more informed and insightful crafter of your own particular mode of reflective believing as you move toward increased proficiency in the reflective arts.

The Advanced Beginner

While there is no ceremonial bestowal of an embossed certificate that documents our progression from novice to advanced beginner, there are some markers that chart our transition across this and the other admittedly permeable boundaries proposed by the Dreyfus brothers. These indicators are analogous to those that chart the progress in other art forms such as musical composition or architectural design. The novice phase in musical composition as taught in universities and conservatories in this country, for example, requires a student to develop some proficiency in understanding the standard harmonic language and forms of Western music. Such understanding is manifest by the performative ability to compose in imitation of these styles. Thus, it is common to require composition students to write a motet in the style of Palestrina (d. 1594) or a fugue in the style of J. S. Bach (d. 1750).

Similarly, architectural students are often required to replicate the sketches of classical architects such as those found in *The Four Books of Architecture* by Andrea Palladio (d. 1580). Interestingly enough, Palladio himself was replicating designs from the ancient Roman architect Vitruvius (d. c. 15 BCE). This replicating exercise is akin to the process I proposed above for beginners in the reflective arts (i.e., learning a "classical" form of theological reflection, and exercising that form with some diligence and care).

The move from novice to advanced beginner often continues to involve a good deal of imitation—whether that is in musical composition or the reflective arts. Increasingly, however, personal creativity and improvisation comes to shape the art. This was certainly a path I often took when first teaching the form of TR invented by James and Evelyn Whitehead. For example, after becoming somewhat adept at their model and method I was challenged by the previously cited work of my colleague Stephen Bevans, who convincingly demonstrated how context was a much richer framework than culture (see textbox 5.1). Thus, I substituted context as described by Bevans for the conversation partner the Whiteheads had designated "culture." Next, I experienced some pushback from students, especially a few of them from Asia, about the "assertion" move, which sounded unnecessarily aggressive to them. It is at that point that I began playing with the "stewing" metaphor that I employed in the previous chapter. Mary Frohlich, a colleague who teaches in the

TEXTBOX 5.1

"First, context includes the experiences of a person's or group's personal life. . . . Second, personal or communal experience is only possible within the context of culture. . . . Third, we can speak of context in terms of a person's or a community's 'social location' . . . (i.e.) whether one is male or female, rich or poor, from North America or Latin America, at the center or at the margins of power. . . . Finally, the notion of present experience in our context involves the reality of social change." (Bevans 2005, 5–6) area of spirituality, wondered whether the well-attested spiritual discipline of discernment might be an even better way of naming this stage. The voice that the Whiteheads designated as "tradition" was also experienced as increasingly confining, with its exclusive emphasis on Christian sources. When students—such as one Christian pastor who had ministered for ten years among Muslim communities in Pakistan—tried to respect other religious resources such as the Qur'an within the framework of the Whiteheads, it appeared that this holy book could only be relegated to the "cultural" voice rather than be treated as a religious resource in their model.

While I was still employing the fundamental structure of the Whiteheads, honoring their three-voiced model and a progression of three basic rules guiding the conversation, the multiple substitutions that I was making as an advanced beginner were markers of increased originality and imagination. That process would continue as, for example, I was introduced to the management style known as appreciative inquiry. Different from a problem-solving approach, which often focuses on what is wrong with an institution, appreciative inquiry holds that institutions need methods of inquiry that uncover the "ordinary magic, beauty and real possibility of organization life" (Ludema 2001, 5). Thus, I began to wonder how one might engage in the reflective arts in an appreciative rather than problem-solving mode.

The stage of an advanced beginner implicitly admits that most of us are not initially capable of creation *ex nihilo* (i.e., "out of nothing"). Nonetheless, this is an inventive stage in which we are invited to take the method or methods we have previously explored with some thoroughness and begin to deconstruct and reconstruct them. Imagine possible other moves or voices, and experiment substituting dialogue partners or processes born of your own context or further study. If you are from a Wesleyan tradition, for example, you might be inspired to engage what Albert Outler called the "Wesleyan Quadrilateral" (Outler 1985) or those four sources that John Wesley employed in his theological reasoning: scripture, tradition, reason, and experience, with scripture clearly being the most important of those. Since this quadrilateral is a collection of "voices" with no explicit parallel method, one could wed them to Cardijn's "see-judge-act" or the Whiteheads' "attend-assert-pastoral response" in the construction of a hybrid model and method in Wesleyan mode.

The options are virtually unlimited in this stage that invites serious experimentation. Every experiment, of course, will not produce a work of art, and some of our efforts will be less than successful and maybe even minor disasters. However, such negative evidence is valuable and helps us play the game of reflective believing increasingly more effectively, as we learn what not to do in particular contexts or in various moments of the reflective believing process. This rich and quite conscious dynamic of imagining, substituting, deconstructing, and creating is the work of the advanced beginner, and when exercised consistently and critically—often through trial and error—it poises us eventually to emerge as a competent actor.

The Competent Actor

I have never been very good at other languages, although I have spent years studying them, including four years of Latin and two years of German at the high school level. Multiple courses in French, Greek, German, and even more Latin followed, but despite my best efforts, I have always seemed to remain at what I would consider the advanced beginner stage with other languages. My litmus test for making that judgment is my consistent inability to think in another language; instead, I find that I am usually working hard at translating in my head. Many colleagues who are gifted linguists and can think not only across languages but also in multiple languages are often a source of not-so-holy envy for me.

Maybe even more astounding for me have been some of the graduate students from around the world that I have had the privilege of teaching and coaching in preaching and worship leadership. One in particular comes to mind. His first language was Arabic, but he had also learned Hebrew at an early age. When he joined a Roman Catholic religious community he was sent to Germany for a year of initial formation, and so picked up his third language. Upon completion of that training he came to the United States for his graduate work with us in English. He took the presiding course with me in his fourth year of study and performed the requisite ritual leadership and preaching in his fourth language with great grace and intelligence. Way beyond the point of reading prayer texts out of some official book, this was very intelligent internalization of the rite and texts matched with marked fluency in English. He was amazing.

The reason I take this small excursion into languages—and my unabashed envy of the multilingual among us—is because I find it an apt analogy and accessible framework for thinking about what it means to move from the stage of an advanced beginner to a competent actor. Advanced beginners can often function well in another language environment: reading road signs, ordering dinner at a restaurant, and negotiating with store clerks or street vendors. That is not, however, the same as true competency in a language. At this third stage as I envision it in linguistic mode, the dictionary is all but abandoned, there is marked fluency not only in "classroom discourse" but also in the language of the street, and the exhausting practice of translating in one's head has all but subsided. This linguistic competency is really an entry into the world of authentic bilingualism.

This is not a fluency everyone achieves, whether that is in languages or the language game of reflective believing—yet it is one for which we strive. In the reflective arts, similar to the language arts, the practitioner at this stage is moving beyond an explicit reliance on guidebooks, rules, and processes. More study and experimentation is still ahead and skills can further be refined. At the same time, there has been so much internalization achieved by this point that—like my Arabic-Hebrew-German-English-speaking student—operating in another language is largely instinctive, although occasionally it is necessary to call to mind some rule of grammar or ask a friend the meaning of an unfamiliar word or phrase.

Besides fluency, another marker of the transition from advanced beginner to competent actor—particularly in regard to reflective believing—is a growing degree of originality in both shaping and negotiating this evolving language game. As noted above, advanced beginners need to experiment and exercise their improvisational skills as they shape a model of reflective believing that is appropriate for their own way of believing. This is particularly important at this stage in our shared history, for there are virtually no explicit models for this form of discourse. The distinction between an advanced beginner and a competent actor, however, is one who has taken that experimentation and originality to a point where something truly new emerges.

Originality, of course, is a quite disputed concept, especially in this current era, marked at least in my own country by so many public disputes about intellectual property rights and patent infringements. In an earlier age, originality was not so much creation *ex nihilo* but such a particular and unique take on previous existing material that something distinctive and new emerged. There is probably no greater example of this in Western art than the English poet and playwright William Shakespeare (d. 1616). His legendary gift for borrowing preexistent material was so expansive that Shakespearean scholar Geoffrey Bullough (1966–1975) could publish a monumental eight-volume work documenting those many sources.

For our own purposes here, we could examine the shared praxis method of Thomas Groome (see appendix 1A) and demonstrate how he took the work of Paulo Freire and crafted something quite new out of it. Similarly, we might consider Holland and Henriot's reliance on Cardijn that nevertheless produced a framework as original as the pastoral circle (see appendix 1B). On the other hand, these models could be symbolic of their authors' long-time study and experience that actually brought them to the level of advanced proficiency and expertise. Earlier in their individual journeys their experimentation brought them to the level of competency, and there are obviously traces of that in their writings. Yet these distinctive contributions heralded in quite celebrated publications no longer appear to be the work of competent actors but the most advanced of reflective practitioners. Thus, with her permission, I will illustrate this competency stage with the imaginative and original work of an esteemed former student (appendix 1E).

Christina Zaker came to our Ecumenical Doctor of Ministry program with rich experience as a Roman Catholic pastoral minister and practitioner of the reflective arts. Well trained in various "classical" methods of TR, she was also well versed in a decidedly Christian-Catholic form of biblical spirituality. In her biblical training she was particularly struck by the power and possibilities of the gospel parables for ministerial reflection. Those who follow trends in Christian biblical studies recognize how much parabolic discourse has become an increasingly rich treasure for theologians in my tradition.

What intrigued Christina was the element of surprise in the Christian New Testament parables. Dominic Crossan has been a pivotal voice in helping Christians to reimagine the power of parables. Many of us through Sunday worship have listened to gospel proclamations of parables and sometimes pedestrian preaching on those texts that have deflated them, turned them into unwelcome moments of moralizing, and sapped their subversive dynamic. When taken seriously, however, parables have a sort of "pull-the-rug-out-from-under-you" dynamic. Akin to the Charlie Brown comic strip we described in chapter 4, or the best of both comedy and tragedy, they create enough familiarity to invite you into their house, and then pose sufficient disruption that the house you thought you knew is now quite upside down.

Christina capitalized on this disruptive yet revelatory potential of parables and, in an imaginative and original move, wondered what would happen to traditional forms of TR if they were done in parabolic mode. While the other "classical" forms of TR would undoubtedly allow for surprise, they did not embrace it as a contributory as well as transformative element. In some ways, this move is analogous to what chemists have taught us for centuries about catalysts. For example, from organic chemistry we understand that certain elements like hydrogen and oxygen easily combine when exposed to each other and become water or H_2O. On the other hand, those who understand chemistry also explain to us that certain elements only combine when some new catalyst makes them "dance" together (e.g., high temperature, increased pressure, or some metal or other catalytic compound).

In an analogous way, Christina not only inserted parable in the reflective process—as a novice or more probably an advanced believer might do—but, in a decidedly non-beginner's move, she also took seriously parable as a catalyst that could change the entire chemistry of the process. Thus, while admittedly in conversation with Killen and de Beer, the Whiteheads, Groome, and others, she employed the category of parable as a terrain-shifting reactant for reimagining TR in a unique and original way. This reenvisioning was grounded in a series of presuppositions that, while reliant upon others in their individual parts, are original in their wholeness.

Christina's fluency in the well-established language game we call TR, combined with her biblically informed imagination, poised her to do something quite original and contributory. Many of us will not be able to do what she has done in the reflective arts. My hope for my own students is that they eventually become so highly skilled as advanced beginners that, as their intuitive reservoir expands, they might edge toward a kind of blessed competency in the many years ahead of them in ministry. It is not my experience, however, that most ministerial students will achieve the level of fluency and imagination that allows them to be Christina's peers in TR. While I have permission to use something of Christina's work, and chose to position her at the level of competent actor, I do not presume she will stay there. Her original contribution of TR in parabolic mode actually revealed that she was already working at a level of advanced competency and well on her way to proficiency and beyond.

A little reality check here: in the Dreyfus brothers' schema competency seems to be only a middling state, a moderately acceptable level from which one needs to push off into proficiency in the pursuit of expertise. On the other hand, I consider ministerial competency as a useful norm. Given our reflections in chapter 4 on the integrative juggling that chaplaincy, pastoring, or other forms of spiritual leadership require, maintaining a dynamic competency across that demanding spectrum of orthopathy, orthopraxis, and orthodoxy is quite a feat and a worthy goal. My personal concern is not about our ministerial graduates who will not become experts but about those obvious few who launch into ministry as novices or struggle at the stage of advanced beginners throughout their pastoral service.

The Proficient Practitioner

As we progress upward through the Dreyfus brothers' model, the air gets a little more rarified and the stages increasingly difficult to describe adequately. While it is somewhat easier to outline the differences between a novice and an advanced beginner, or even advanced beginner and competent actor, the hair-splitting becomes more challenging as one moves into the lofty realm of proficiency. This might be especially true for spiritual practices such as reflective believing, which concern themselves with skills surrounding the very nature of human transcendence or what some would consider skills crafted for broaching the divine. These transcending capacities are not readily quantifiable, as one might clock the speed of a pitcher's fast ball or establish a golfer's handicap.

This is not to say that proficiency itself is rare. On the contrary, while not always recognized, it is all around us. There are highly proficient individuals who can figure out what is wrong with our cars or computers after only a few moments under the hood or at the keyboard. At your favorite restaurant, gifted sous-chefs can deliver that amazing pasta in the marinara sauce and follow it up with a tiramisu that might make your Italian grandmother jealous. Consider all of those highly proficient builders, carpenters, plumbers, and painters who designed, constructed, and finished your home, office, or school. And then there are the armies of dedicated and gifted educators who teach toddlers to read, help students in primary school conquer the basics of math, inspire future scientists in junior high school with inventive experiments and online learning, and plant the love of learning in students of every age. As an educator, my first instinct would be to explain, or at least illustrate, the difference between a competent actor and a proficient professional through examples from my own world of theological education. On the other hand, that might be a little self-serving and potentially deadly dull. If this is to be an imaginative journey, let's try an unexpected path.

In vacation spots and large public squares throughout the Western world, one quite often encounters street artists. There are jugglers, mimes, and waves of musicians of unending variety, each attempting to pry you loose from a few pesos, euros, or dollars. One group that consistently intrigues me—from the plaza outside the Pompidou Center in Paris to Navy Pier in Chicago—are the caricature artists who publicize their uncanny abilities to capture your likeness while exploiting visible facets of the real you rendered as a once-in-a-lifetime sketch.

There are many things that fascinate me about these facile practitioners, and elements of their well-honed craft that help me imagine what proficiency might look like in the reflective arts. First of all, they are amazing, nimble, and sometimes downright speedy. Most can turn out a full body caricature, often with splashes of color, in six or seven minutes. Incredibly, they exercise this artistic speed in a public arena, often with friends or other potential customers looking on, so there is certainly pressure to produce a quality product. They also have to walk that fine line between being too bland, so that the end product really doesn't look like a caricature, and visually exploiting the client's nose or ears to such a degree that the customer is miffed or even insulted. Their originality is tested with every client, since every face is different. Admittedly, there are some clichés that can be repeated, or patterns to exploit, but the caricature has to look like an original interpretation of the person sitting in front of them at this very moment. To top it all off, they are often plying their craft in an environment in which they are flanked, if not surrounded, by a host of other caricature artists. Talk about putting your livelihood on the line!

In an analogous way those who have acquired proficiency in the reflective tasks—often something we see in our most influential mentors—have to be on their toes as well. After years of discipline, study, and practice they now instinctively recognize that no experience is repeatable, no moment identical to one either they or we have previously experienced. Like the pre-Socratic philosopher Heraclitus (d. 475 BCE), they understand that you never step in the same river twice, and that every human is a unique stream of ever-changing life. This requires the proficient to be nimble, and also sometimes to act very quickly. When such a mentor encounters a novice or advanced beginner, a group of disciples or strangers who are perplexed or under duress, they cannot simply reschedule the group or individual to come back in two weeks so as to have sufficient time for engineering a proper response. Proficiency in the reflective arts is clearly a well-tuned imagination and ethically honed intuition on the line.

When casting around for an example of this quick, imaginative, and gifted immediacy I was reminded of a particular story of a dear colleague who lost her battle with breast cancer a few years ago. The story was related by our mutual friend, Herbert Anderson. One of the first women to be ordained by the Lutheran Church in this country, Connie Kleingartner (d. 2008) was a pastor, educator, and eventually professor and field education supervisor at the Lutheran School of Theology in Chicago. She also taught leadership in our Ecumenical Doctor of Ministry program for many years. While she was serving a small congregation in Iowa, she began a support group for women who had experienced sexual violence. One of the women in the group, no matter how much she talked, could never feel free from the contamination resulting from that violence. The woman repeatedly talked about how "dirty" she felt. A gifted symbolic reflector, my friend invited the woman into a private shower facility, where she scrubbed her and scrubbed her and scrubbed her. After much soap, water, and tears, a slow transformation occurred, and the woman could begin to feel that physically, psychologically, and spiritually she was on her way to feeling clean and whole again.

There is no method, course, or book—certainly not this one—that is going to provide a path to that kind of emotionally brilliant and spiritually profound form of improvisation. Like a fresh face newly seated in front of a caricature artist on the Atlantic boardwalk, novices and even advanced beginners in the reflective arts want and expect something never before seen. The Christian scriptures allude to this when St. Paul talks about "becoming a new creation" (2 Cor. 5:17). Those proficient in the reflective arts display such creativity at a profound level. This gift, however, is not the self-centered performance of some diva in search of adulation but the self-effacing charism of a wise spirit willing to be emptied so that others might flourish.

And how does one achieve such proficiency? It certainly is not assured no matter what path we choose or gurus we follow. Obviously wisdom of this sort also cannot develop without expending significant time and energy in practicing the reflective arts. But there is more. It also requires the kinds of knowledge we examined in chapter 4, in which head smarts and heart gifts and body instincts dance deeply with each other. Maybe an especially important, though not always welcome, ingredient essential to this level of reflective proficiency is suffering. While that might sound odd to some, many spiritual traditions offer us images of inordinately wise leaders—from Buddha to Jesus, and Abraham to Mohammed—whose wisdom was forged in the crucible of suffering. As previously noted, chemistry teaches us that certain elements only combine when some new catalyst makes them "dance" together. My wager is on suffering as an indispensible catalyst for allowing time and knowledge, experience and empathy, head skills and hand skills, to give rise to this quality of reflective art.

The Expert

Anyone who is well acquainted with the work of the Dreyfus brothers recognizes that I am proposing a much steeper incline on the path from novice to expert than they imagined or intended. As noted at the outset of this chapter, their original work with the United States Air Force was designed not only to discover how some jet pilots became experts at their craft but also to construct training programs that would consistently produce pilots with such expertise. I do not believe such is possible within the reflective arts. It is akin, in my own religious tradition, to creating a formation program with the stated purpose of leading people into advanced holiness and producing saints. That just does not happen.

Since I can propose neither a path to sanctity nor one to expertise in the art of reflective believing, this could appear to be a futile few paragraphs in a chapter with decreasing value or viability. There may be, however, some hidden promise in examining this loftiest of stages in the reflective arts. Returning to Alain de Botton and his very smart book *Religion for Atheists*, I am bolstered by his discussion of "role models." In this *Non-Believer's Guide to the Uses of Religion*, de Botton admits how important is our desire and need to mimic others while recognizing that our lives are not always populated with the people whom we could or should emulate (see textbox 5.2). Then, with

TEXTBOX 5.2

"Among the few hundred people we regularly encounter, not very many are likely to be the sorts of exceptional individuals who exhaust our imagination with their good qualities, who strengthen our soul and whose voices we want consciously to adopt to bolster our best impulses." (de Botton 2012, 91)

some holy envy, he talks about how Catholicism offers its followers thousands of "saints" whose qualities are worth emulating.

While not suggesting that experts in the reflective arts are "saints," it makes sense to consider them as models worthy of emulation. In my own tradition, while it is expected that we imitate the saints, there is little expectation that such imitation will lead to our own canonization. In a parallel move, maybe imitating the lofty examples of true experts in the reflective arts might help to rescue us from a life as novices in this adventure.

As for examples who seem to inhabit this elevated level of expertise with great consistency, my first thought was the comedian Robin Williams (d. 2014). This may be a bit of a bizarre exemplar, especially in view of his struggles with drug and alcohol addictions as well as serious bouts with depression that seems to have contributed to his unexpected and tragic death in 2014. I am certainly not proposing Williams as some saint who provides us with a template for living. On the other hand, it is not as a moral model but as a rarified practitioner of the comedic arts that persuades me to consider Williams here as an apogee of the Dreyfus brothers' progression. He had few, if any, peers in his field: an opinion echoed by so many entertainment professionals after his death.

In January 2001 Williams was interviewed by James Lipton on the TV series *Inside the Actors Studio* (Williams 2008). This exhilarating and exhausting romp is, in some ways, an accidental documentary on the very nature of expertise. Williams is virtually uncontainable by the host as he blitzes through one accent after another, morphs from character to character, and plays his audience like Yo-Yo Ma plays his 1712 Stradivarius cello. Even before he gets on stage, Lipton admits that trying to categorize Williams is akin to capturing lightning with a butterfly net. Williams does not disappoint.

One of the most enlightening moments comes about thirty-seven minutes into the program—long after the host has recognized that he actually only has a butterfly net and Williams is a frenetic electric charge. The instigation is Lipton referencing a previous interview with Williams's friend and comedic colleague, Billy Crystal. In that interview, Lipton asked Crystal if there was anyone he envied. Crystal waxed eloquent about Williams's gifts, particularly the speed of his improvisational responses. Lipton then asks Williams a series of rapid-fire questions: "How do you explain the mental reflexes that you are deploying tonight with such awesome speed? Are you thinking faster than the rest of us? What the hell is going on?" Predictably, the audience explodes in applause, and just as predictably, Williams does not offer a dissertation on his comedic agility. Instead, he launches into a four-minute improvisational display, employing a scarf absconded from an unsuspecting member of the audience, and models that which cannot be put into words. Williams's dazzling embodiment beyond explanation is reminiscent of the nineteenth-century musical master Franz Liszt. It is reported that once, after playing an etude, someone asked him what the piece meant. Liszt purportedly said nothing and simply sat back down at the keyboard and played the piece again.

No program inspired by the Dreyfus brothers' model can predict, much less ensure, the emergence of another comedic genius like Robin Williams. The same may be even more true for a master of the reflective arts such as Tenzin Gyatso, the fourteenth Dalai Lama. Deeply rooted in his own tradition of Tibetan Buddhism known as the Gelug school, His Holiness also possesses a comprehensive knowledge across the breadth of Buddhist history and teachings that positions him as the foremost living Buddhist teacher on the planet. That in itself would qualify him for admission to the elite status of expert in the reflective arts. Yet, as with other venerable guides, he is so much more.

Most admirable and challenging for me is his startling ability to remain profoundly committed to his own form of believing without appearing to be the least bit territorial when it comes to the way others position themselves around religion. As his thinking has evolved, he is not even convinced that religion is the fundamental ground that holds us together. Such provocative thinking has allowed him to reimagine both spirituality and ethics beyond religion (Dalai Lama 2011, xv). Proposing a global ethic that respects the religions of the world without being wed to any of them, His Holiness reveals himself as not only an expert in religiosity but, even more so, one in humanity. It is our common humanity which he believes truly binds us together.

Part of the mastery on display in shaping this dialogue from humanity is the spectrum of conversation partners the Dalai Lama is able to muster and even master. Ranging across Eastern and Western philosophies, his writings and teachings are peppered with insights from subatomic physics, cosmology, ancient languages such as Sanskrit, and quantum mechanics. Not simply an esoteric dabbler, His Holiness is such a respected dialogue partner in this regard that in 2010 the Stanford School of Medicine invited him to participate in a conference on the neuroscience of compassion.

Yet, as with any true expert in the reflective arts, this is not simply a great mind at work, but also an embodied compassion that radiates hope. His daily study is matched by hours of meditation. Robin Williams kept his audiences rolling in the aisles; the Dalai Lama keeps people in respectful dialogue to promote harmony. Honored by millions as a manifestation of the Bodhisattva of compassion, he has been richly acknowledged as the very embodiment of his beliefs, including the 1989 Nobel Peace Prize for his nonviolent advocacy for the liberation of Tibet.

Along with compassion, one of the most continuous themes in His Holiness's teaching concerns suffering. It is something he has profoundly experienced in his own life—including his own flight into exile in 1959—and he often notes that our experience of suffering is a central way in which all human beings are connected to each other. It is a way that he stays deeply connected with the people of Tibet in their persecution, and with a tradition that he sadly notes may be coming to an end. It is possible that he will be the last Dalai Lama the world has known. While the vast majority of us will never attain his status of reflective expertise, his invitation to compassion in suffering and to embrace our common humanity connects us to his spirit and empowers us in that same spirit to nourish each other.

Epilogue
Gifts for the Journey

Not I, not any one else can travel that road for you,
You must travel it for yourself.
It is not far, it is within reach,
Perhaps you have been on it since you were born and did not know,
Perhaps it is everywhere on water and on land.

—*Walt Whitman (2008, no. 46)*

It was not an especially long transatlantic flight—only from London to Chicago. Yet, as I sat in the waiting area, the flight was long enough to prod me to ponder with more attentiveness than usual who might be seated close to me. I needed to get some writing done and hoped that there would be sufficient quiet in the cabin to do so. While in the lounge, I noticed a young father with an infant daughter. He was agile with her as he grabbed the front of her pajamas and hoisted her out of her baby seat and into his arms for the trip. I was in coach but have traveled enough that I wrangled a pretty good seat in the very front of the economy section on the aisle: 12G, to be exact. I was praying that Dad and his lovely daughter were somewhere south of row 24. As it happened, they ended up in 11H: kitty-corner across the aisle. I was grateful that I had packed both ear plugs and my noise-reducing headphones.

When I had completed my mental checklist, decided that all would be well, and was braced for the journey, in walked Jeremy with a five-month-old strapped to his chest and a two-and-a-half-year-old on his arm. They occupied the three seats directly in front of me. I had images of the transatlantic flight from hell. As Jeremy good-naturedly attempted to wrestle the luggage, the children, and himself into place, the woman sitting next to me—whom I later learned was originally from Juarez, Mexico—looked up and asked, "Do you want me to hold the baby?" Without missing a beat, Jeremy unstrapped Charlie and transferred him into the arms of an adoring stranger.

Charlie was only five months old. I guessed he was older, but his father later admitted that he was a big boy, very active and quite happy. He bounced on Maria's lap dozens of times while Maria laughed and chatted with Jeremy about how she had traveled cross country with her daughter when she was a baby. The daughter, sitting next to her, was now a beautiful teenager who said nothing, but smiled broadly at her mother's remembrances. Jeremy was so understated, Charlie so cute, and the almost-three-year-old so difficult that I knew I had to collaborate and somewhat reluctantly offered to be Maria's back-up.

A few thousand miles into the trip Charlie became my responsibility. I had read enough educational theory to know that he would be happier if I turned him away from me, and so I put a slide show of pictures on my computer resting in front of him on my tray table. Charlie spent lots of time bouncing, grabbing for the pictures, and leaning across the aisle chortling to a genial traveler reading a newspaper. Charlie seemed especially interested in the sports section. He eventually wore himself out, and when Jeremy took him back, he quickly fell asleep.

Ethan was another story all together: he was a walking advertisement for every theory about the "terrible twos." Ethan battled his father at almost every turn, while Dad showed little exasperation with the tyke and his many outbursts. Often these were resolved relatively quickly by Jeremy digging into his "magic bag." It seems that a friend had bought, wrapped, and packed eighteen small presents for Ethan to keep him occupied during the transit from London to Los Angeles that—including the Chicago layover—would last about eighteen hours: what a smart friend! As we chatted, it became clear that Ethan was not only a temperamental two-year-old but also grieving. His mother had died four months ago, a month after Charlie's birth. This newly shaped family of three was traveling to the west coast to visit Jeremy's father, a trip symbolic of the long road of grieving that lay ahead for them.

The draft of this monograph was virtually finished before I made that trip. There was only a yet-to-be-written conclusion or epilogue that friends who had been reading previous versions suggested that it needed. I left it unwritten, not that I imagined it would be long or taxing to compose; it is just that, while one of the shortest monographs I have produced, it felt like the well was running dry. Since returning from my trip, however, the well seemed replenished. It has been difficult to get that traveling threesome out of my mind (or heart) and have been regularly reflecting on that once-in-a-lifetime encounter. I have also reconnected with Jeremy and his band of merry men. From time to time he sends me pictures of Charlie and Ethan as they grow, and has graciously allowed me to recount this story for you. In that process, some wisdom has revealed itself that has resonance with the journey that led to this writing. They might also strike a sympathetic chord in you.

While this book was not initially conceived to be a personal reflection on my own trek into ministry or envisioned as a kind of self-manifesto on theological education, some of that has occurred. It seems that my confession in chapter 1 that "this is personal" was more prophetic than imagined. Jeremy and his life-giving children reminded me how many gifts I have been given on that journey: maybe you have as well. Some I have opened too quickly, like a petulant toddler needing a fresh distraction or an aging educator desperate for new ideas in a course that needed crafting or an article past its deadline. Other gifts, like those colored markers that kept captivating Ethan's attention throughout the flight, have nourished me many times over. Evelyn and Jim Whitehead's wisdom and friendship, like that of my coauthor and friend Herbert Anderson, are enduring examples of such gifts for me; you probably have your own. Take a moment of reflective believing and remember, then cherish them, and maybe even tell them what a gift they have been. I am also reminded and even a little startled how much my family of origin has been both a source and a sounding board for this reflective journey. This writing has prompted me to tell them that again.

There have also been quite unexpected gifts like those parables that Christina Zaker warned us about in chapter 5, whose treasure was sometimes only grudgingly and belatedly recognized. If I had possessed some magic wand at the beginning of that London to Chicago flight, I would have instantaneously waved it so that the two Brits and their multiple babies would have been seated in different sections, or maybe even booked on different flights. Looking back, I would have been the poorer for such facetious wand waving. Analogously, I have been blessed with a galaxy of students and colleagues who, usually unintentionally, have pulled the rug out from under me and served as catalysts for reimagined and renewed believing. The attempt to craft some order out of that ensuing chaos has been its own revelation. I hope you encounter such parables on your own chaordic journey, and maybe practice more humility in recognizing their value than I have.

Ethan, Charlie, and Jeremy also remind me how much grieving there has been on this journey for me. Beloved colleagues have moved on, moved away, retired, or died. Students for whom I considered myself a special mentor faded from view or sought out other mentors. Prized initiatives in which I invested head, hand, and heart were sometimes transformed in ways beyond my liking, or became unsustainable beyond my will. And then there are the lost or squandered opportunities that haunt me like the poet's "road less traveled," and whose path I chose to ignore. You may have similar grief in your own life, no matter at what stage you are in your reflective journey. While often unwelcome, they are not without promise, and are often a crucible that distills a kind of wisdom to nudge us out of novitiate or the plateau of advanced beginner into the promise of becoming a more competent actor in the reflective arts.

Relating the incident of this grieving trio of travelers also underscores for me anew how incomparable is the narrative lens in practicing the reflective arts. The story weaving of characters and setting, feelings and events, shared sorrows and cradled babies—more than some abstract list of lessons learned or checklist of tasks on our beeping calendars—powerfully symbolizes the integrating dance of heart, hand, and head that reflective believing both requires and paradoxically nurtures. Attempting to craft this story as a way to honor and respect those events, while at the same time attempting to make it accessible to those who did not have the privilege of being on flight AA97 and sitting in our section of the plane, is a complex form of improvisation that needs to be both engaging and ethical.

Maybe, most of all, that traveling threesome cautioned me that as this writing project comes to a conclusion, the journey does not. My pilgrimage into the reflective arts—one that somewhat reluctantly took the road less traveled into reimagined believing—still stretches out before me. Your journey will be different from mine, just as Jeremy (who knew his wife for a dozen years), Ethan (who knew his mother for only two), and Charlie (who will have no living memory of her) each have their own path of grieving and healing and loving before them. My hope is that, in the spirit of the Buddhist parable we related in chapter 4, this book has been a helpful raft to you, aiding you to reach whatever shore is on your horizon. It is offered as a gift for your journey, as you in turn will be gifts to others as they take up the challenging and enlightening path of reflective believing.

Appendix 1

1A: THOMAS GROOME

Primary Texts

Groome, Thomas. 1975. "Toward a Theory/Method of Liberation Catechesis." Ed.D. diss., Columbia University Teacher's College.

———. 1980. *Christian Religious Education: Sharing Our Story and Vision.* San Francisco: Harper & Row.

———. 1987. "Theology on Our Feet." In *Formation and Reflection: The Promise of Practical Theology*, edited by Lewis Mudge and James Poling, 55–78. Minneapolis, MN: Augsburg.

———. 1991. *Sharing Faith: A Comprehensive Approach to Religious Education and Pastoral Ministry.* San Francisco: HarperSanFrancisco, 1991.

———. 2011. *Will There Be Faith?* New York: HarperCollins, 2012.

Definition

"Shared Christian Praxis is a participative and dialogical pedagogy in which people reflect critically on their own historical agency in time and place and on their sociocultural reality, have access together to Christian Story/Vision, and personally appropriate it in community with the creative intent of renewed praxis in Christian faith toward God's reign for all creation" (Groome 1980, 135).

Major Influences

- Paulo Freire's liberative approach to education that rejected any "banking model" of depositing knowledge in students; more specifically, Freire's idea of a "generative theme" in his 1970 *Pedagogy of the Oppressed* (New York: Herder and Herder).
- Jurgen Habermas's work on the importance of critical reflection on social praxis that unmasks ideologies that legitimate repression and lead to emancipatory ways of living (e.g., his 1971 *Knowledge and Human Interests*, translated by Jeremy J. Shapiro [Boston: Beacon Press]).
- Dwayne Heubner, Groome's doctoral advisor at Columbia, especially his concept of making the Christian story and vision *accessible* central to Groome's Movement 3. See his 1999 *The Lure of the Transcendent: Collected Essays by Dwayne E. Huebner*, edited by Vikki Hillis (Mahwah, NJ: Lawrence Erlbaum).

Outline of Method

- This is an approach to educating people in the Christian faith enacted through a focusing activity and five subsequent pedagogical movements. The language of "movement" implies that this is a free-flowing process. While there is a logical sequence to the movements, in practice they often overlap, recur, and recombine in other sequences (Groome 1991, 146).
- *Focusing Activity:* This activity establishes a focus for the curriculum by engaging people in a generative theme that creates a shared sense of understanding of the nature of this educational event. It can take the form of a symbolic presentation or event (e.g., storytelling or a dance), or even inviting people to reflect upon some common aspect of their current context (e.g., homelessness, unemployment in their area) (Groome 1991, 155).
- *Movement 1: Naming/Expressing "Present Praxis":* This movement invites participants to express their own understandings, feelings, beliefs, and so forth around the particular theme that has been introduced and symbolized in the focusing activity. This expression can take the place of a discussion or any other form of expression, such as writing or miming (Groome 1991, 175).
- *Movement 2: Critical Reflection on Present Praxis:* This movement encourages participants to reflect critically on the "present action" that was the focus of Movement 1 by considering such things as the assumptions be-

hind that practice as well as its sociohistorical roots. It is meant to enable participants to appropriate critically the present praxis in their own context (Groome 1991, 187).

- *Movement 3: Encounter with the Christian Story and Vision*: This movement is intended to make accessible elements from the Christian story and vision that are appropriate to the generative theme central to the learning event. The "story" indicates the faith tradition of the Christian community as expressed in scripture, doctrines, rituals, spiritualities, and so forth. The "vision" points to the promises and demands that the story makes on Christians (Groome 1991, 215).
- *Movement 4: A Dialectical Hermeneutic between Praxis and Story/Vision*: The design of this movement is for participants to place their critical reflection on present praxis that emerged from Movements 1 and 2 in critical dialogue with the Christian story/vision that was explored in Movement 3. The intent is twofold: both a critique of present praxis in light of the Christian story/vision and a critique of the Christian story/vision in light of present praxis. The goal of this dialogue is to enable participants to think about living more faithfully (Groome 1991, 249).
- *Movement 5: Decision/Response for Lived Christian Faith*: This movement is an invitation for participants to make specific decisions about how to live their faith in the world. Such decisions can be personal choices by each participant, or a communal decision that the group achieves through a consensus process (Groome 1991, 266).

Commendations

- The process nature of this approach allows for flexibility in the shaping and sequencing of the movements.
- It respects the learners as subjects and agents in this reflective process (Groome 1991, 86).
- It recognizes that such a process is cognitive and also engages the body, emotions, and the will (Groome 1991, 87).
- It respects the religious heritage of Christians (Groome 1991, 90).
- It takes the context seriously (Groome 1991, 98).
- Participants are moved to decision making and action.
- It acknowledges the communal nature of this reflective work.
- The individual's agency is respected in making decisions for action.

Recommendations

- The framework is decidedly Christian and would need serious adaptation to be useful in other contexts of believing.
- While the steps themselves are relatively simple, the framing language and explanations are highly philosophical and sometimes mask the applicability of this process.
- Its educational framework may make it less helpful for other formational or spiritual forms of reflection.

Related Bibliography

Bezzina, Michael. 1997. "Does Groome's Shared Praxis Provide a Sound Basis for Religious Education?" *Word in Life: Journal of Religions Education* 45:16–24.

Charter, Miriam. 1994. "Thomas H. Groome's Shared Praxis Approach to Ministry: Questioning Its Application in the Protestant Evangelical Church." *Trinity Journal* 15:89–113.

Devenish, Philip. 1994. "Book Reviews." *Journal of Religion* 74:276–77.

Kinast, Robert. 2000. "A Ministerial Style of Theological Reflection." In *What Are They Saying about Theological Reflection?*, 16–20. Mahwah, NJ: Paulist.

Wong, Arch Chee, et al. 2009. "Learning through Shared Christian Praxis: Reflective Practice in the Classroom." *Teaching Theology & Religion* 12:305–20.

1B: JOE HOLLAND AND PETER HENRIOT

Primary Texts

Deberri, Edward, James Hug, Peter Henriot, and Michael Schultheis. 1985. *Our Best Kept Secret: The Rich Heritage of Catholic Social Teaching*. Washington, DC: Center of Concern.

Holland, Joe, and Peter Henriot. 1983. *Social Analysis: Linking Faith and Justice*. Rev. ed. Maryknoll, NY: Orbis.

Definition

Theological reflection is "an effort to understand more broadly and deeply the analyzed experience in the light of living faith, scripture, church social teaching and the resources of the tradition" (Holland and Henriot 1983, 9).

Purpose

"The purpose of this study is . . . to describe the task of social analysis and its relevance to social justice action, to provide illustrations of analytical approaches to various problems, and to explore the suggestions and questions they raise for pastoral responses" (Holland and Henriot 1983, 4).

Major Influences

- Joseph Cardijn's "see, judge, act" method with its inductive emphasis on beginning with human experience and discerning the frameworks embedded in that experience, from his 1914 "Hoe kan een studiekring werken naar buiten?" accessed September 29, 2014, http://www.josephcardijn.com/1914---how-does-a-study-circle-work.
- Juan Luis Segundo's hermeneutical circle in his 1976 *The Liberation of Theology* (Maryknoll, NY: Orbis).
- Key principles of modern Catholic social teaching—for example, the link between Christian faith and the promotion of justice, and the option for the poor (Holland and Henriot 1983, 4).

Outline of Process

- This process involves a series of four "movements" that represent the close relationships between four mediations of experience, which they call the "pastoral circle" (Holland and Henriot 1983, 7).
- Begins with *insertion*, which locates the "geography" of the pastoral responses in the lived experience of individuals and communities (Holland and Henriot 1983, 8):
  - It considers what people are feeling, what they are undergoing, and how they are responding.
  - This constitutes the primary data for the community's insertion into the experience.
  - It asks key questions such as (Holland and Henriot 1983, 9):
    - Where and with whom are we locating ourselves as we begin the process?
    - Whose experience is being considered and discussed?
    - Whose experience is being left out?
    - Does the experience of the poor and oppressed have a privileged role to play in the process?

- Step two is the *social analysis* "which examines cause, probes consequences, delineates linkages, and identifies actors. It helps make sense of experiences by putting them into a broader picture and drawing the connections between them" (Holland and Henriot 1983, 8).
  - At this stage it is important to examine which analytical tradition is being followed in the analysis,
  - to ask if there are any presuppositions in these analyses that need to be tested,
  - and to ask if it is possible to use a particular analysis without agreeing with its accompanying ideology (Holland and Henriot 1983, 9).
- Step three is *theological reflection*, which is "an effort to understand more broadly and deeply the analyzed experience in the light of living faith, scripture, church social teaching and the resources of the tradition. The word of God brought to bear upon the situation raises new questions, suggests new insights, and opens new responses" (Holland and Henriot 1983, 9).
  - It examines what methodological assumptions underlie the theological reflection.
  - The relationship between the social analysis and theology must also be considered (e.g., is the analysis in a complementary or subordinate position to theology).
  - Also important is a consideration of how resonant the theology is with the existing social situation (Holland and Henriot 1983, 10).
- Step four, *pastoral planning*, involves the acts of deciding and acting (Holland and Henriot 1983, 10).
  - This is the fundamental purpose and goal of the pastoral circle.
  - It is based on the previous analysis and reflection and asks what response is now necessary for both individuals and communities to make.
  - There is also a design responsibility at this stage, shaping the response so that it is the most effective in both the short and the long term.
  - Key questions at this stage include:
    - Who participates in the pastoral planning process?
    - What is the relationship between those who "serve" and those who are "served" by this process?
    - What are the implications of the very process that is employed for making these responses?

- This is not so much a "circle" as a self-admitted "spiral" recognizing that the process gives rise to new experiences, which are the starting point for breaking new ground, a process that has no "final" conclusion (Holland and Henriot 1983, 9).

Commendations

- The process consistently asks presuppositional questions about the methods being employed whether those are theological or sociological, recognizing that no method is neutral and affects the outcome. The authors are also quite upfront about their own presuppositions and biases (Holland and Henriot 1983, 5).
- There is an implicit recognition that local issues or experiences are linked to larger systems that must be analyzed for an appropriate response.
- Analysis and reflection is always for the sake of some action.
- There is a particular concern for the marginalized and powerless (i.e., an "option for the poor") (Holland and Henriot 1983, 5).
- There is an explicit reliance on the rich and often underutilized body of teaching known as Catholic social teaching.

Recommendations

- The reliance on Roman Catholic teaching as both a primary motivation and a resource makes its adaptation in other traditions problematic.
- The authors themselves recognize the limits of social analysis as a tool for social change (e.g., it can be perceived as a negative and elitist tool) (Holland and Henriot 1983, 90–91).
- Because of its focus on changing social and political structures, it is less useful for individuals or groups more concerned about their interior spiritual journey.
- The approach to theological reflection is underdeveloped in comparison to the attention given to social analysis.

Related Bibliography

Ambrogi, Thomas. 1985. "Social Analysis: Linking Faith and Justice." *Religion and Intellectual Life* 2:104–7.

Holland, Joe. 2003. *Modern Catholic Social Teaching, 1740–2000: The Popes Confront the Industrial Age 1740–1958*. Mahwah, NJ: Paulist Press.

Wijsen, Frans. 1997. "The Pastoral Circle in the Training of Church Ministries." *Afer* 39:238–50.

Wijsen, Frans, Peter Henriot, and Rodrigo Mejia, eds. 2005. *The Pastoral Circle Revisited: A Critical Quest for Truth and Transformation*. Maryknoll, NY: Orbis.

1C: PATRICIA O'CONNELL KILLEN AND JOHN DE BEER
Primary Texts

Killen, Patricia O'Connell, and John de Beer. 1983. "'Everyday Theology': A Model for Religious and Theological Education." *Chicago Studies* 22:191–206.

———. 1995. *The Art of Theological Reflection*. New York: Crossroad.

Killen, Patricia O'Connell. 1995. "Assisting Adults to Think Theologically." In *Method in Ministry: Theological Reflection and Christian Ministry*, by James D. Whitehead and Evelyn Eaton Whitehead, 103–11. Rev. ed. Kansas City, MO: Sheed & Ward.

Definition
"Theological reflection is the discipline of exploring individual and corporate experience in conversation with the wisdom of a religious heritage. The conversation is a genuine dialogue that seeks to hear from our own beliefs, actions and perspectives, as well as those of the tradition. It respects the integrity of both. Theological reflection therefore may confirm, challenge, clarify and expand how we understand our own experience and how we understand the religious tradition. The outcome is new truth and meaning for living" (Killen and de Beer 1995, viii).

Major Influences
- John Dunne (e.g., his emphasis on having an affective connection to an issue and his idea to employ images as the way to get to the heart of the matter in his 1978 *Reasons of the Heart: A Journey into Solitude and Back Again into the Human Circle* [New York: Macmillan]).
- Bernard Lonergan's concept and method for moving toward insight in his 1957 *Insight: A Study of Human Understanding* (London: Longmans, Green).
- John Shea's narrative approach to theological reflection and its emphasis on human experience (e.g., his 1978 *Stories of God: An Unauthorized Biography* [Chicago: Thomas More Press]).

- David Tracy's work on engaging classical texts and heritage in his 1981 *The Analogical Imagination: Christian Theology and the Culture of Pluralism* (New York: Crossroad).

Outline of the Method

- The method is based on what the authors consider to be a five-part human process for coming to wisdom or "meaning making," each part related to the others in a circular spiral (Killen and de Beer 1995, 20):
  - enter your experience through a nonjudgmental narration or description of it (Killen and de Beer 1995, 25);
  - encounter your feelings,
    - feelings are our embodied affective and intelligent responses to reality as we encounter it (Killen and de Beer 1995, 27);
  - paying attention to feelings allows images to arise;
  - considering and questioning images may spark insight;
  - if you are willing, insight can lead to action (Killen and de Beer 1995, 21).
- It requires a standpoint of exploration (Killen and de Beer 1995, 16)
  - rather than a standpoint of certitude in which we see the unfamiliar only in terms of what we already believe (Killen and de Beer 1995, 5),
  - or a standpoint of self-assurance in which we decided to trust only ourselves, our own experience, and how we think and feel in each new situation (Killen and de Beer 1995, 10).
- The framework for theological reflection is rooted in the human process for coming to wisdom;
  - it also encompasses expanding the definition of "experience" so that it includes four elements:
    - action or our lived narrative (Killen and de Beer 1995, 54);
    - religious tradition, including scriptures, doctrinal teachings, stories of denominational heroes and heroines, saints, church history, official church documents, and the like (Killen and de Beer 1995, 55);
    - culture, which has three distinctive parts:
      - culture, narrowly defined, including the symbols, mores, assumptions, values, sciences, artifacts and philosophies of human groups (Killen and de Beer 1995, 56);
      - the patterns of organized interaction within human groups or social structures; and
      - the physical environment (Killen and de Beer 1995, 57);

- positions, or those attitudes, opinions, beliefs, and convictions that one holds and is willing to defend in argument (Killen and de Beer 1995, 58).
- It also always includes four elements and processes:
  - focusing on some aspect of experience (Killen and de Beer 1995, 68);
  - describing that experience to identify the heart of the matter;
  - exploring the heart of the matter in conversation with the wisdom of the Christian heritage (Killen and de Beer 1995, 69);
  - identifying from this conversation new truths and meanings for living (Killen and de Beer 1995, 69).
  - The movement toward insight and the framework for theological reflection are quite similar. The key differences lies in part three (i.e., how the heart of the matter or focal point from experience is considered). In the framework for theological reflection the heart of the matter is considered in light the Christian heritage (Killen and de Beer 1995, 74).

Commendations

- It begins with the human process of coming to insight.
- There is a concern for wisdom and not simply problem solving.
- Feeling and imagination often play a key role.
- The concept of "culture" is thickened (e.g., its three parts noted above).
- There is clear flexibility as to the beginning point (e.g., they offer nine possible processes illustrating this [Killen and de Beer 1995, 87–109]).

Recommendations

- The emphasis on feelings could render the process somewhat individualistic.
- While expanded, the concept of culture is yet monolithic and somewhat static (e.g., references to "our first world culture" [Killen and de Beer 1995, 31]).
- The definition of experience is so broad that it seems to collect virtually all data under that rubric, including scientific and philosophical theories (Killen and de Beer 1995, 56).
- More suited to egocentric contexts, with emphasis on individual experience, and maybe less resonant with sociocentric contexts and group experience.

Related Bibliography

Kinast, Robert. "A Spiritual Wisdom Style of Theological Reflection." In *What Are They Saying about Theological Reflection?*, 20–26. Mahwah, NJ: Paulist.

Neuman, Matthias. 1995. "The Art of Theological Reflection." *Horizons* 22:313–14.

Thompson, Judith, Stephen Pattison, and Ross Thompson. 2008. *SCM Studyguide to Theological Reflection*, 65–67. London: SCM Press, 2008.

1D: JAMES AND EVELYN WHITEHEAD

Primary Texts

Whitehead, James D., and Evelyn Eaton Whitehead. 1975. "Educational Models in Field Education." *Theological Education* 11:269–78.

———. 1980. *Method in Ministry: Theological Reflection and Christian Ministry*. San Francisco: HarperSanFrancisco.

———. 1995. *Method in Ministry: Theological Reflection and Christian Ministry*. Rev. ed. Kansas City, MO: Sheed & Ward.

Definition

Theological reflection in ministry is the process of bringing to bear in the practical decision of ministry the resources of Christian faith (Whitehead and Whitehead 1995, ix), a systematic way to approach the various sources of religious information that leads not just to theoretical insight but also to pastoral decision and action (Whitehead and Whitehead 1995, x).

Major Influences

- David Tracy, especially his correlational method and focus on common human experience in his 1975 *Blessed Rage for Order* (New York: Seabury).
- Gerard Egan's paradigms of listening and asserting in his 1975 *The Skilled Helper* (Monterey, CA: Brooks/Cole).
- Bernard Lonergan's understanding of method from his 1972 *Method in Theology* (New York: Herder and Herder).
- Anne Carr's overview and analysis of theological method in Rahner in her 1977 *The Theological Method of Karl Rahner* (Missoula, MT: Scholars Press).

Outline of Method

- They distinguish between a model, and a method.
- The model points to three key sources of information relevant to decision making in ministry (Whitehead and Whitehead 1995, ix), or the "voices" in the conversation (Whitehead and Whitehead 1995, 4):

○ The Christian tradition: the massive range of insight and grace that scripture and Christian history provide (Whitehead and Whitehead 1995, 6), including rituals, doctrines, and acts of piety (Whitehead and Whitehead 1995, 23).

○ Experience: the ideas, feelings, biases, and insights that individuals and communities bring to reflection (Whitehead and Whitehead 1995, 43).

○ Cultural resources: employing Clifford Geertz's definition of culture as "an historically transmitted pattern of meanings embodied in symbols . . . by means of which persons communicate, perpetuate and develop their knowledge about and attitudes toward life" (Whitehead and Whitehead 1995, 56).

- The method describes the process by which the conversation proceeds (Whitehead and Whitehead 1995, 5):

○ Attending: seeking out the information on a particular pastoral concern available in experience, tradition, and cultural sources; this requires listening critically while suspending judgment (Whitehead and Whitehead 1995, 13).

○ Asserting: bringing the perspectives from the three sources into a lively dialogue of mutual clarification in order to expand and enrich religious insight; this requires the courage to share convictions as well as a willingness to be challenged (Whitehead and Whitehead 1995, 13).

○ Pastoral response: moving from discussion and insight to decision and action; this requires discerning how to respond, planning the response, and evaluating how the response was done (Whitehead and Whitehead 1995, 13).

Commendations

- The distinction between model and method as a way to consider theological reflection as a conversation that requires defined conversation partners.
- Serious push to "befriend" the Christian tradition (Whitehead and Whitehead 1995, 9).
- Recognition of the pluriformity of the tradition (Whitehead and Whitehead 1995, 7) and that it carries a history of both grace and malpractice (Whitehead and Whitehead 1995, 8).
- Emphasis on the communal nature of theological reflection (Whitehead and Whitehead 1995, xiii).
- The shaping of a method that is practical, accessible, and adaptable.

- Experience is the starting point of reflection (Whitehead and Whitehead 1995, 9).
- The introduction of culture as a critical element in theological reflection.

Recommendations

- Tradition is decidedly Christian, with little place for other faith traditions, or spiritual heritages, and seems to preclude any canon of virtues or principles that humanists might bring to reflection.
- Culture is presented in a somewhat modernistic manner that does not address the dynamics of gender, age cohort, social location, and so forth. Context (e.g., as defined by Stephen Bevans in chapter 5) is a richer concept.
- The language of assertion could signal permission for assertive behavior, rather than a stance of discernment, reflective "stewing" or other metaphors for allowing the three sources to interact effectively with each other.
- There is an intentional ministerial focus here, well suited to problem solving; it seems less suited for personal growth in wisdom, virtue, or holiness.

Related Bibliography

Graham, Elaine, Heather Walton, and Frances Ward. 2005. *Theological Reflection: Methods*, 161–63. London: SCM Press.

Kinast, Robert. "A Ministerial Style of Theological Reflection." In *What Are They Saying about Theological Reflection?*, 6–14. Mahwah, NJ: Paulist.

Zilles-Soberano, Jane. 1982. "Method in Ministry: Theological Reflection and Christian Ministry." *Religious Education* 77:119–20.

1E: CHRISTINA ZAKER

Primary Text

Zaker, Christina. 2012. "Theological Reflection in Parabolic Mode." D.Min. thesis, Catholic Theological Union.

Definition

Theological reflection in parabolic mode is a process which invites participants "to explore where God's movements can be found in their daily lives and to understand how that grace is inviting transformation" (Zaker 2012, 105).

Major Influences

- John Dominic Crossan's understanding of myth and parable in his 1975 *The Dark Interval: Towards a Theology of Story* (Niles, IL: Argus).
- Joe Holland and Peter Henriot's emphasis on listening to the margins in their 1983 *Social Analysis: Linking Faith and Justice*, rev. ed. (Maryknoll, NY: Orbis), 9.
- Patricia O'Connell Killen's course on theological reflection at Loyola University in 1991 (and subsequent publication with John de Beer; see appendix 1C), especially her focus on a spiritual wisdom style of theological reflection.
- William Herzog's consideration of parables as "codification" for stimulating social analysis in his 1994 *Parables as Subversive Speech: Jesus as Pedagogue of the Oppressed* (Louisville, KY: Westminster/John Knox Press).
- Edward Schillebeeckx's concept of Jesus as the parable of God (e.g., in his 1980 *Christ: The Experience of Jesus as Lord* [New York: Seabury]).
- James and Evelyn Whitehead's method for how to do theological reflection.

Outline of Method

- There are eight foundational presuppositions that are presented to participants and discussed by them and further clarified where needed before the process begins (Zaker 2012, 105):
  - God is present throughout our lives.
  - Parables have a reference point with the gospel image of the "kingdom of God."
  - Parables offer good news for the marginalized.
  - Parables have aspects that are familiar, comforting, that make sense.
  - Parables have aspects that are surprising or shocking and challenging.
  - Parables are open-ended—waiting for a response.
  - It is helpful to be open to the process.
  - It is helpful to have a community willing to discern together and to challenge one another.
- The process itself involves six steps (Zaker 2012, 105–9):
  - Naming the experience: Rooted in the first foundational assumption that God is present through people's lives, participants are encouraged to explore any story from their lives as a way to begin discerning God's presence and offer it as a community reflection.

○ Exploring the experience as a community: Grounded in assumptions 7 and 8 about openness and community, the listening community is invited to look for connections between this particular story and their own lives as well as the stories of believers related in the gospels and gospel parables, looking for both similarities and differences.

○ Recognizing the familiar: Resonant with assumption 4, this step invites participants to ask a series of questions to help them recognize the familiar in their own stories and begin to ponder why these threads look familiar or feel comfortable.

○ Seeing the surprise: Based on assumption 5, participants are then encouraged to first identify what was surprising in the stories and then begin to explore why this was so.

○ Acknowledging the invitation: This stage has a twofold movement, rooted in assumptions 2 and 3: first is to invite the "observer-participants" to consider where God might be acting in the experience and what kind of response that might invite; second is to welcome those who were part of the original experience to consider how their actions might both have acknowledged and contributed to the building up of God's reign, particularly on behalf of the marginalized.

○ Responding to the invitation: This final stage is an invitation for participants to internalize these reflections and ponder how they will hold on to them, and how such reflections might encourage them to recognize God in their daily lives and respond.

Commendations

- The process is designed for ordinary believers and requires no formal religious or theological training.
- There is a structured didactic moment (the eight assumptions) that provides participants some common ground for the ensuing process.
- Human experience is affirmed as the stuff of theological reflection.
- The narrative quality of the process is inclusive as all people have stories.
- Individual experience is respected, but it is also offered as a gift for community reflection and harvesting.
- There is a unique focus on a particular part of the Christian heritage (parables) that goes to the heart of the gospels and Jesus' own speech pattern.

Recommendations

- The assumptive world for this enterprise is thoroughly Christian, and may be inaccessible to people who believe in other ways.
- Even within the Christian heritage, there is not only a gospel focus but also a parable focus which may not engage those many Christians who do not root their faith in the Bible.
- While respecting the interplay between individual and communal stories, the emphasis on commonalities might contribute to a kind of narrative homogenization that blurs the particularities of the social location of each storyteller.

Appendix 2

A Funeral Tribute to Michael Grometer from His Uncle Ed, March 16, 2013

I hope you'll excuse me if I read this; it will help ensure that I will more easily get through it. My instinct for this moment in the service would, of course, be to read something from scripture, maybe a gospel story about resurrection or one of Paul's letters confirming the promise of eternal life. That is always a source of consolation for me. I know, however, that it was not always such for Michael, who had his own canon of wisdom and inspiration. At the center of that canon of music and movies, science and fiction were the writings of J. R. R. Tolkien. His mother read *The Hobbit* to him when he was four, and they worked through all three volumes of *Lord of the Rings* by the time he was six. When he was in fourth grade, he tried to check the latter out of the library at his school, but they wouldn't let him. When he told his mother about this, she asked him why he did that since he owned the whole thing. He responded that the school required him to check one book out of the library every week and that was the only one he wanted. Not surprisingly, the various films of the series by Peter Jackson were favorites of Michael's and much of the rest of this side of the family, and the new productions of *The Hobbit* were anticipated as though each was Christmas and Easter all rolled into one.

What I do not remember speaking to Michael about is the amount of literature written about Tolkien as a Catholic-Christian author and even theologian. Tolkien himself attested to the profound influence that his faith had on these literary works. Late in 1953, a priest friend of the Tolkien family read *The Lord of the Rings* shortly before it was published and wrote to Tolkien, suggesting that the image of Queen Galadriel was really the Virgin Mary. Tolkien wrote back, agreeing with the comparison and further noted that his own perception of beauty was founded on his images of Mary. I think Michael's grandmother, Tiffany, would be pleased with that revelation. Tolkien closed his letter by writing, "*The Lord of the Rings* is of course a fundamentally religious and Catholic work; unconsciously so at first, but consciously in the revision" (Tolkien 1995).

One of the most obvious Christian themes in Tolkien's writings is the resurrection of Gandalf, who had to sacrifice everything—even his efforts and very hopes that the dark lord might be defeated—in order to secure the safety of the fellowship. The fellowship itself, like a fictional communion of saints or unlikely band of disciples, had its own theological overtones.

Michael well understood the importance of fellowship. I've been viewing many pictures of him these past few days, and Michael never seemed happier than with his own fellowship, with Candice and Brigit, his family—especially his brother Mark—the cousins, Joe, and his many friends and, of course, a beer. Michael was fiercely loyal to his fellowship, and in the end he even seems to have sacrificed everything on a quest to help one of them.

This past week, like family in the shire, we have been waiting for him to come home. Of course, we have waited for him before. His mother reminded me that before his birth she was in labor for thirty hours with him, and then the only way to bring him into the light was to have an emergency caesarian section. She concluded that sometimes Michael made things unnecessarily difficult—often as a way to underscore their or his importance.

The last time we waited almost seven years for Michael to return home. This time from prison. It was a long and difficult journey, a monthly road trip by mother and grandmother and occasionally others to support and encourage him on the more difficult journey into himself. A journey into discipline and soul searching, and ultimately a journey to freedom marked by that glorious limo ride with Candice, Mark and the cousins, his mother and maternal grandmother, and me, into the beginning of a new life.

But maybe like Frodo, Michael was never really settled. The wounds never quite healed, the Shire never really home, and his restless spirit never completely calmed. And so we have waited for him to come home a last time, again in a limo—Michael always had style—but now as part of his final journey "into the west." And in that final journey he leaves this beloved fellowship behind: Brigit and Candice, Taf and Tony, Mark and his grandparents, so many cousins, relatives, and friends; a fellowship more brokenhearted than Sam or Merry or Pippin as they stood on that mythical shore, for unlike them, we never had a chance to look into his eyes a final time, to tell him how much we loved him, or have that last, memorable enduring embrace and kiss.

We are deeply grieved because he was taken from us so quickly, yet even in this past week we have also smiled, even laughed through our tears recalling his antics and posturing, his charming contrariness and impish intelligence, and his prophetic insistence that when it came to saying good-bye, he wanted an Irish wake—now to be realized on the eve of St. Patrick's Day—he did have a knack for getting his way. And in these treasured memories we are both saddened and consoled by a life lived too briefly, but also one lived so fully, so distinctively, and so wholeheartedly.

And so with full hearts we launch Michael into his final journey, into the fellowship of those who have gone before him, where I believe with all my heart that Tiffany and Jim and Dale were waiting there on the other shore to guide him and greet him when he passed over into that eternal Valinor.

Last Sunday, Candice told Brigit the difficult news that her father, like her great-grandmother before him, had become an angel, a special light in the heavens, someone to watch over her, protect her, and guide her: Michael the angel, or, according to the ancient legends, Michael the archangel. Who understands the mind of a child or knows the inner heart of a four-year-old, but in the ensuing conversation with the gathered relatives and friends Brigit announced that she, too, wanted to be an angel, something we gently suggested would take her many, many years.

We also are on a journey, to be protectors and guides to the innocent and the lost, and in quest of our own metaphorical wings. As we move forward with this gaping hole in our fellowship, we remember with abiding love our own archangel Michael who illumined life for us in his unique and incomparable way, and in the tradition in which he was baptized pray a variation on those ancient words for this journey: Michael, may your fellow angels take you into paradise, and may Gandalf come to welcome you, and lead you to the holy city, the new and eternal Valinor. Rest in peace, Michael. Rest in peace.

References

"An Array of Errors." 2011. *The Economist*, September 10. Accessed April 4, 2013. http://www.economist.com/node/21528593.

Anderson, Herbert, and Edward Foley. 1997. *Mighty Stories, Dangerous Rituals: The Intersection of Worship and Pastoral Care*. San Francisco: Jossey-Bass.

Aristotle. 2000. *Nichomachean Ethics*. Edited and translated by Roger Crisp. Cambridge: Cambridge University Press.

Augsburger, David. 1986. *Pastoral Counseling across Cultures*. Philadelphia: Westminster Press.

Bauman, Zygmunt. 2000. *Liquid Modernity*. Cambridge: Polity Press.

Beaudoin, Tom. 1998. *Virtual Faith: The Irreverent Spiritual Question of Generation X*. San Francisco: Jossey-Bass.

Benedict XVI. 2006. "Regensburg Address." Accessed February 15, 2013. http://www.zenit.org/en/articles/papal-address-at-university-of-regensburg.

Benne, Robert. 1995. *The Paradoxical Vision: A Public Theology for the Twenty-First Century*. Minneapolis, MN: Fortress.

Bereza, Jan M. 2004. "Christian-Buddhist Dialogue: A Contemporary Phenomenon." *Dialogue & Universalism* 14:25–29.

Bergson, Henri. 1988. *Matter and Memory: Essay on the Relationship of Body to Spirit.* Translated by Nancy Margaret Paul and W. Scott Palmer. New York: Zone Books.

Bernhard, Andrew. 2012. "How *The Gospel of Jesus's Wife* Might Have Been Forged: A Tentative Proposal." Accessed April 5, 2013. http://www.gospels.net/gjw/mighthavebeenforged.pdf.

Bevans, Stephen. 2005. *Models of Contextual Theology.* Rev. ed. Maryknoll, NY: Orbis Books.

Bordo, Susan. 1989. "The Body and the Reproduction of Femininity." In *Gender/Body/Knowledge: Feminist Reconstructions of Being and Knowing*, edited by Alison Jaggar and Susan Bordo, 13–33. New Brunswick, NJ: Rutgers University Press.

Bourdieu, Pierre. 1998. *Practical Reason.* Stanford, CA: Stanford University Press.

Brachear, Manya A. 2012. "Muslims Bypass Mormons as Fastest-Growing Religion in Illinois." *Chicago Tribune*, May 2. Accessed March 19, 2013. http://www.chicagotribune.com/news/local/breaking/chi-religious-census-independent-evangelicals-one-of-the-largest-religious-groups-20120501,0,6368818.story.

Brookfield, Stephen. 2012. *Teaching for Critical Thinking: Tools and Techniques to Help Students Question Their Assumptions.* San Francisco: Jossey-Bass.

Bullough, Geoffrey. 1966–1975. *Narrative and Dramatic Sources of Shakespeare.* 8 volumes. London: Routledge & Kegan Paul.

Burroughs, Augusten. 2002. *Running with Scissors.* New York: St. Martin's Press.

Cahalan, Kathleen. 2012. "Integration in Theological Education." In *The Wiley-Blackwell Companion to Practical Theology*, edited by Bonnie J. Miller-McLemore, 386–95. Chichester, West Sussex, UK: Blackwell Publishing.

Cardijn, Joseph. 1914. "Hoe kan een studiekring werken naar buiten?" Accessed September 29, 2014. http://www.josephcardijn.com/1914---how-does-a-study-circle-work.

Carr, Wesley. 1997. *Handbook of Pastoral Studies.* London: SPCK.

Clapper, Gregory. 1990. "*Orthokardia*: The Practical Theology of John Wesley's Heart Religion." *Quarterly Review* 10:49–66.

Collins, Jim. 2005. "Level 5 Leadership: The Triumph of Humility and Fierce Resolve." *Harvard Business Review* 83:136–46.

Collins, Raymond F. 1984. *Models of Theological Reflection.* Lanham, MD: University Press of America.

"A Common Word between Us and You." 2007. Accessed February 15, 2013. http://
www.acommonword.com/the-acw-document/.

Crossan, John Dominic. 1975. *The Dark Interval: Towards a Theology of Story*. Niles,
IL: Argus Publications.

Dalai Lama. 2011. *Beyond Religion: Ethics for a Whole World*. New York: Houghton
Mifflin Harcourt.

de Botton, Alain. 2012. *Religion for Atheists: A Non-Believer's Guide to the Uses of
Religion*. New York: Vintage Books.

Deleuze, Gilles, and Félix Guattari. 1988. *A Thousand Plateaus*. Translated by Brian
Massumi. New York: Continuum.

Dhammapada. 1985. Translated into English by Dharma Publishing Staff. Oakland,
CA: Dharma Press.

Dreyfus, Hubert L., and Stuart E. Dreyfus. 1980. "A Five Stage Model of the Mental
Activities Involved in Directed Skill Acquisition." Accessed September 29, 2014.
http://www.dtic.mil/get-tr-doc/pdf?AD=ADA084551.

———. 1986. *Mind over Machine: The Power of Human Intuition and Expertise in the
Era of the Computer*. New York: Free Press.

Dreyfus, Stuart E. 2004. "The Five-Stage Model of Adult Skill Acquisition." *Bulletin
of Science, Technology & Society* 24:177–81.

Dupuche, John. 2013. "An Interfaith Ashram: A Description." *Dialogue Interreligieux
Monastique* 3. Accessed April 14, 2013. http://www.dimmid.org/index.asp?Type=B
_BASIC&SEC={D959726F-C9A3-4F14-B6EC-795A67B9C7BD}.

Dulles, Avery. 1974. *Models of the Church: A Critical Assessment of the Church and
Its Aspects*. Garden City, NY: Doubleday.

Durant, Will. 1926. *The Story of Philosophy: The Lives and Opinions of the World's
Greatest Philosophers*. New York: Simon & Schuster.

Ferris, Timothy. 2005. *The Whole Shebang: A State of the Universe(s) Report*. New
York: Simon & Schuster.

Foley, Edward. 2014. "Reflective Believing: Reimagining Theological Reflection in an
Age of Diversity." *Reflective Practice: Formation & Supervision in Ministry* 34:60–75.

———. 2012. "Ritual Theory." In *Wiley-Blackwell Companions to Religion: A
Companion to Practical Theology*, edited by Bonnie Miller-McLemore, 143–52.
Oxford: Blackwell Publishing.

Freire, Paulo. 1970. *Pedagogy of the Oppressed*. New York: Herder and Herder.

Gyatso, Tenzin. 2005. "Our Faith in Science." *New York Times*, November 12. Accessed December 16, 2013. http://www.nytimes.com/2005/11/12/opinion/12dalai.html?pagewanted=all.

Hanh, Thich Nhat. 2007. *Living Buddha, Living Christ*. 10th anniversary ed. New York: Riverhead Books.

Heifetz, Ronald, and Marty Linsky. 2002. *Leadership on the Line: Staying Alive through the Dangers of Leading*. Boston: Harvard Business School Press.

Hitchens, Christopher. 2007. *God Is Not Great: How Religion Poisons Everything*. New York: Twelve.

Hock, Dee. 1995. "The Chaordic Organization: Out of Control and Into Order." *World Business Academy Perspectives* 9:5–18. Accessed September 22, 2014. http://www.ratical.org/many_worlds/ChaordicOrg.pdf.

Holland, Joe, and Peter Henriot. 2006. *Social Analysis: Linking Faith and Justice*. Maryknoll, NY: Orbis Books.

Hooper Virtual Paleological Museum. 2013. Accessed May 13. http://park.org/Canada/Museum/insects/evolution/evolution.html.

Huffington Post. 2013. "Pope Francis Says Atheists Who Do Good Are Redeemed, Not Just Catholics." May 22. Accessed October 6, 2014. http://www.huffingtonpost.com/2013/05/22/pope-francis-good-atheists_n_3320757.html.

Jackson, Wes. 2005. "Toward an Ignorance-Based World View." *The Land Report* 81:14–16. Accessed September 28, 2014. http://www.landinstitute.org/library-post/toward-ignorance-based-world-view-lr81/.

Jung, Carl. 1959. *Archetypes of the Collective Unconscious*. Princeton, NJ: Princeton University Press.

Killen, Patricia O'Connell, and John de Beer. 1994. *The Art of Theological Reflection*. New York: Crossroad.

Kruger, C. Baxter. 2005. *The Great Dance: The Christian Vision Revisited*. Vancouver, British Columbia: Regent College.

Landau, Yehezkel. 2007. "An Interview with Krister Stendahl." *Harvard Divinity Bulletin* 35:29–31.

Langer, Susanne K. 1953. *Feeling and Form.* New York: Charles Scribner.

Lash, Nicholas. 2011. "I Watch My Language in the Presence of God—Theology in the Modern University." Accessed April 4, 2013. http://www.st-edmunds.cam. ac.uk/faraday/Issues_Lash.php.

Lerner, Michael. 2009. "Diversity and a New Bottom Line." *Reflective Practice* 29:108–18.

Ludema, James. 2001. "From Deficit Discourse to Vocabularies of Hope: The Power of Appreciation." In *Appreciative Inquiry,* edited by David Cooperrider, Peter Sorenson, Therese Yaeger, and Diana Whitney, 265–87. Champaign, IL: Stipes Publishing.

Marty, Martin E. 1981. *The Public Church.* New York: Crossroad.

Maslow, Abraham. 1966. *The Psychology of Science.* New York: Harper & Row.

Mehrabian, Albert, and Susan R. Ferris. 1967. "Inference of Attitudes from Nonverbal Communication in Two Channels." *Journal of Consulting Psychology* 31:248–52.

Miller-McLemore, Bonnie. 2004. "Sloppy Mutuality: Just Love for Children and Adults." In *Mutuality Matters: Family, Faith and Just Love,* edited by Herbert Anderson, et al., 121–35. Lanham, MD: Rowman & Littlefield.

Nersessian, Nancy J. 1999. "Model-Based Reasoning in Conceptual Change." In *Model-Based Reasoning in Scientific Discovery,* edited by Lorenzo Magnani, Nancy J. Nersessian, and Paul Thagard, 5–22. New York: Kluwer Academic/Plenum Publishers.

The Network of Spiritual Progressives. 2013. Accessed September 22. http:// spiritualprogressives.org/newsite/.

O'Connor, Thomas St. James, and Elizabeth Meakes. 2008. "Canadian Ethnographic Study of Sources and Definitions of Theological Reflection in Pastoral Care and Counseling." *Journal of Pastoral Care & Counseling* 62:113–26.

Outler, Albert. 1985. "The Wesleyan Quadrilateral in Wesley." *Wesleyan Theological Journal* 20:7–18.

Patel, Eboo. 2012. *Sacred Ground.* Boston: Beacon Press.

Pattison, Stephen, Judith Thompson, and John Green. 2003. "Theological Reflection for the Real World: Time to Think Again." *British Journal of Theological Education* 13:119–31.

Pawlikowski, John. 2003. "Liturgy and the Holocaust: How Do We Worship in an Age of Genocide?" In *Christian Responses to the Holocaust*, edited by Donald Dietrich, 168–76. Syracuse, NY: Syracuse University Press.

Peña, Adolfo. 2010. "The Dreyfus Model of Clinical Problem-Solving Skills Acquisition: A Critical Perspective." *Medical Education Online.* Accessed October 3, 2014. doi: 10.3402/meo.v15i0.4846.

Pew Forum on Religion & Public Life. 2012. "'Nones' on the Rise: One-in-Five Adults Gave No Religious Affiliation." Accessed March 27. http://www .pewforum.org/Unaffiliated/nones-on-the-rise.aspx.

Potok, Chaim. 1981. *The Book of Lights.* New York: Random House.

Prinz, Jesse. 2009. "Is Consciousness Embodied?" In *The Cambridge Handbook of Situated Cognition*, edited by Philip Robbins and Murat Aydede, 419–36. Cambridge, MA: Cambridge University Press.

Rumi, Maulana Jalal al-Din. 2004. "The Three Fish." In *The Essential Rumi*, translated by Coleman Banks, 193–200. New ex. ed. New York: HarperSanFrancisco.

Schipani, Daniel S., and Leah Dawn Bueckert. 2010. *You Welcomed Me: Interfaith Spiritual Care in the Hospital.* Kitchener, Ontario: Pandora Press.

Shah-Kazemi, Reza. 2010. "God, 'The Loving.'" In *A Common Word: Muslims and Christians on Loving God and Neighbor*, edited by Miroslav Volf, Ghazi bin Muhammad, Prince of Jordon, and Melissa Yarrington, 88–109. Grand Rapids, MI: Eerdmans.

Short, Robert L. 1990. *Short Meditations on the Bible and Peanuts.* Louisville, KY: Westminster John Knox.

Spivak, Gayatri Chakravorty. 2005. "Postcolonial Theory and Literature." In *New Dictionary of the History of Ideas*, edited by Maryanne Cline Horowitz, 5:1859–67. Detroit: Charles Scribner's Sons.

Stedman, Chris. 2012. *Faitheist: How an Atheist Found Common Ground with the Religious.* Boston: Beacon Press.

Steinberg, Saul. 1976. "View of the World from 9th Avenue." *New Yorker*, March 29. Accessed October 2, 2014. http://archives.newyorker.com/?i=1976-03-29#folio=CV1.

Thompson, Judith. 2008. *SCM Studyguide to Theological Reflection*. London: SCM Press.

Tolkein, J. R. R. 1995. *The Letters of J. R. R. Tolkein*, edited by Humphrey Carpenter. Boston: Houghton Mifflin.

Toolan, David S. 1993. "Chicago's Parliament of the World's Religions." *America* 169/8:3–4.

Tracy, David. 1983. "The Foundations of Practical Theology." In *Practical Theology*, edited by Don Browning, 61–82. San Francisco: Harper & Row.

Univision. 2014. "Voice of the People." Accessed September 27, 2014. http://www.univision.com/interactivos/openpage/2014-02-06/la-voz-del-pueblo-matriz-1.

Vatican Council II: The Basic Sixteen Documents. 1996. Edited by Austin Flannery. Northport, NY: Costello.

Volf, Miroslav, Ghazi bin Muhammad, Prince of Jordan, and Melissa Yarrington, eds. 2010. *A Common Word: Muslims and Christians on Loving God and Neighbor*. Grand Rapids, MI: Eerdmans.

Waldrop, M. Mitchell. 1996. "The Trillion-Dollar Vision of Dee Hock: The Corporate Radical Who Organized Visa Wants to Dis-organize Your Company." Accessed July 18, 2013. http://www.fastcompany.com/27333/trillion-dollar-vision-dee-hock.

Ward, Pete. 2002. *Liquid Church*. Peabody, MA: Henrickson Publishers; Carlisle, Cumbria, UK: Paternoster Press.

Wesley, Carr. 1997. *Handbook of Pastoral Studies*. London: SPCK.

Wesley, John. 1987. *The Appeals to Men of Reason and Religion and Certain Related Open Letters*, edited by Gerald Cragg. Vol. 11 of *The Works of John Wesley*. Nashville, TN: Abingdon Press.

Whitehead, James D., and Evelyn Eaton Whitehead. 1995. *Method in Ministry: Theological Reflection and Christian Ministry*. Rev. ed. Kansas City, MO: Sheed & Ward.

Whitman, Walt. 2008. *Leaves of Grass*. A Project Gutenberg EBook. Accessed October 3, 2014. http://www.gutenberg.org/files/1322/1322-h/1322-h.htm.

Wiesel, Elie. 1966. *The Gates of the Forest*. New York: Holt, Rinehart and Winston.

Wiggins, Grant, and Jay McTighe. 2005. *Understanding by Design*. 2nd ed. Upper Saddle River, NJ: Pearson Education, Inc.

Williams, Robin. 2008. *Inside the Actors Studio: Robin Williams*. Universal Music & Video Distribution.

Wittgenstein, Ludwig. 2009. *Philosophical Investigations*. Rev. 4th ed. Edited by Gertrude Anscombe, Peter Hacker, and Joachim Schulte. Chichester, West Sussex, UK: Wiley-Blackwell.

Wolfteich, Claire. 2011. "Reclaiming Sabbath as Transforming Practice: Critical Reflections in Light of Jewish-Christian Dialogue." In *Religion, Diversity and Conflict*, edited by Edward Foley, 265–77. Berlin: LIT Verlag, 2011.

Woolf, Virginia. 1922. *Jacob's Room*. London: Hogarth Press.

World Council of Churches. 1979. Accessed July 23, 2013. http://www.oikoumene .org/en/resources/documents/wcc-programmes/interreligious-dialogue-and-cooperation/interreligious-trust-and-respect/guidelines-on-dialogue-with-people-of-living-faiths-and-ideologies.

Young, William P. 2007. *The Shack*. Newbury Park, CA: Windblown Media.

Zaker, Christina. 2012. "Theological Reflection in Parabolic Mode." D.Min. thesis, Catholic Theological Union.

Index

Abrahamic religions, 4, 7, 29, 85. *See also* Christians; Judaism; Muslims

advanced beginner, 81, 88, 100, 104–7, 108, 110, 111, 113. *See also* Dreyfus, Hubert L. and Stuart E.

affect/affection: Dunne and, 132; holy, 75, 76; Killen and de Beer and, 133; promoting, 73; for strangers, 102; in theologies or spiritualities, 72. *See also* feelings; orthopathy

agnostics: as dialogue partners, 7, 20; statistics about, 15. *See also* atheists

Anderson, Herbert, 32, 39, *40*, 113, 121

appreciative inquiry, 106

arboreal thinking, 11, 63, 83, 87

Aristotle, 71, 74

artists: caricature, 112; and performance, 68; and postcolonial theory, *12*

Assembly of God, *6*, 54

atheists, 67; as dialogue partners, 7, 20; distinguished from "nones," 16; new movement of, 6; statistics about, 15.

See also agnostics; de Botton, Alain; Stedman, Chris

attending, 51; and improvisation, 34; and nonverbal communication, 36; in reflective believing, 33; in ritual, 37. *See also* Whitehead, James and Evelyn

Augsburger, David, 35, 66. *See also* interpathy

Baha'i, *6*, 15

Bauman, Zygmunt, 8–9, 31. *See also* liquid/liquidity

Beaudoin, Tom, 13

beliefs, 9, 28, 48, 71, 88, 98; Buddhists and, 31; Dalai Lama and, 117; dialogue of, with humanists, agnostics, and atheists, 7; diversity of, 19, 26, 29, 31, 53, 89; in Groome, 126; imposing, 37; the Internet and, 13; in Killen and de Beer, 132, 134; reflecting upon, 14; Roman Catholics

and, 85; safeguarding, 26, 32; shared
by Abrahamic religions, 4, 29;
sharing, 24, 26, 36; theologians and,
25. *See also* orthodoxy
believing, 7, 29, 34, 52, 85, 93; alien
forms of, 57, 62, 88, 92; chaordic
nature of, 14; diversity of, 28, 29, 31,
35, 63, 84; from the outside-in, 19–
22; as journey, 69, 122; as mystery,
89; sharing another's way of, 35, 37,
42; shifting contours of, 3, 16, 31, 48.
See also reflective believing
Bevans, Stephen, 3, 105, *105*
Bible. *See* scriptures
body: knowledge, 68, 78, 80, 82, 83;
language, xvi, 36, 93. *See also*
embodiment; orthopraxis
Bordo, Susan, 79, 82
Bourdieu, Pierre, 79–80, 82
Brookfield, Stephen, 87, 88
Buddha, 40, 55, *56*, 68, *86*, 114
Buddhism, 5, 6, 28, *30*, 31, 53–55, 85,
86, 123; in Chicago, 15; Dalai Lama
and, 116; in divinity schools, xv;
and monastic dialogue, 38–39; and
pluriformity, 89; writings, 98. *See also*
Dalai Lama
Bullough, Geoffrey, 109
Burroughs, Augusten, 42

Cahalan, Kathleen, *67*
canon: of beliefs, 88; humanist, 85, 137;
personal, 32, 104, 141
Cardijn, Joseph, 100, 103, 106, 109, 129
Catholicism. *See* Roman Catholic
Catholic Theological Union, 15. *See
also* Ecumenical Doctor of Ministry
program

chaordic: believing, 14; context, xv, xvi,
xvii, 28, 35, 57, 62; leadership, xiii, 11
chaplaincy, xv, 5, 6, 27, 35, 46, 48, 79,
94, 111; interfaith, 53–57
Christians, xiv, 4, 6, 7, 9, 15, 25, 31,
59, 70, 86, 140; faith of, 125, 126,
127; framework for, 128; gospel
of, 58; heritage of, 127, 134, 139,
140; history of, 136; journey of,
86; scriptures of, 72, 97, 100, 104,
113; students, 38, 94, 106; teaching,
70; theology of, 2, 19, 29, 46, 61;
tradition, 84, 106, 127, 136, 137. *See
also* leader/leadership; minister
Church of Jesus Christ of Latter-day
Saints, 6, 75
clinical pastoral education (CPE), 53–55
coach/coaching, 59, 78, 107
Collins, Jim, 74–75
Collins, Raymond, 46, *47*
Comăneci, Nadia, 77–78
comedy. *See* improvisation; Williams,
Robin
common: good, 13, 19, 26, 29, 61, *64*, *81*,
92; ground, 4, 5, 16, 26, 52, 93, 139
Common Word initiative, 4–5
compassion, 73, 117
competent actor, 81, 100, 107–11, 112.
See also Dreyfus, Hubert L. and
Stuart E.
Confucius, 74; values of, 59, 60
context, *xiv*; across, 35, 57, 62, 66, 82;
author's, 31, 82; contemporary, xv,
28; defined, *105*; in the Dreyfus
brothers' frame, *81*; embodied speech
and, 36; insertion into, 61; one's own,
95, 106, 127; postcolonial theory and,
12; religious, 2, 18; small town, 58;

About the Author

Edward Foley is Duns Scotus Professor of Spirituality and the founding director of the Ecumenical Doctor of Ministry program at Catholic Theological Union in Chicago. He is a Capuchin-Franciscan and ordained Roman Catholic priest. An award-winning author, he has produced more than twenty books, translated into multiple languages, including *From Age to Age* and *Mighty Stories, Dangerous Rituals* with Herbert Anderson. A well-known speaker, he has taught in venues such as the University of Chicago and Notre Dame, presented in settings as diverse as the Mayo Clinic and the Houston Astro Dome, and lectured in more than sixty Roman Catholic dioceses from India to the Philippines. He preaches and presides at Old St. Patrick's Church in Chicago.

Made in the USA
Lexington, KY
08 August 2017